Campaign • 157

Trafalgar 1805

Nelson's Crowning Victory

Gregory Fremont-Barnes • Illustrated by Christa Hook

Series editor Lee Johnson

First published in Great Britain in 2005 by Osprey Publishing,
Midland House, West Way, Botley, Oxford OX2 0PH, UK
44-02 23rd St, Suite 219, Long Island City, NY 11101, USA
Email: info@ospreypublishing.com

Osprey Publishing is part of the Osprey Group.

Transferred to digital print on demand 2010

First published 2005
5th impression 2008

Printed and bound by Cadmus Communications, USA

A CIP catalogue record for this book is available from the
British Library

ISBN: 978 1 84176 892 2

Page layout by The Black Spot
Index by David Worthington
Maps by The Map Studio
3D bird's-eye views by Ian Palmer
Originated by PPS-Grasmere, Leeds, UK
Typeset in Helvetica Neue and ITC New Baskerville

Author's note

Please note that even among naval architects and historians,
variations exist in the spellings of some ships' features and
types, e.g. quarter deck/quarterdeck; mizzen
mast/mizzenmast; ship of the line/ship-of-the-line;
fore mast/foremast; round shot/roundshot; grape
shot/grapeshot etc.

Numbers that follow a ship's name indicate her rating, i.e.
the number of guns she mounted. Thus: *Swiftsure*, 74.

Bird's-eye views: Readers should be aware that while the
approximate position of the ships is known, the condition of
their sails at any given point is not. Moreover, frequently
changing conditions, e.g. strength and direction of the wind,
ocean current, damage aloft, and variations in ships' courses,
render impossible a perfectly accurate representation of the
sails employed at any given time. As a compromise, a
standard model is employed for all vessels, modified where
damage is known.

Artist's note

Readers may care to note that the original paintings from which
the colour plates in this book were prepared are available for
private sale. All reproduction copyright whatsoever is retained
by the Publishers. All enquiries should be addressed to:

Scorpio
158 Mill Road
Hailsham
East Sussex
BN27 2SH
UK

Email: scorpiopaintings@btinternet.com

The Publishers regret that they can enter into no
correspondence upon this matter.

The Woodland Trust

Osprey Publishing is supporting the Woodland Trust, the UK's
leading woodland conservation charity, by funding the
dedication of trees.

www.ospreypublishing.com

Key to military symbols

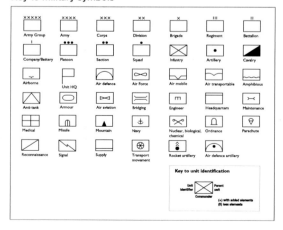

Trafalgar 1805

Nelson's Crowning Victory

CONTENTS

Battle of Trafalgar. The last great naval action fought under sail, Trafalgar marked the beginning of a century of British maritime supremacy and opened the way for a small island nation to achieve commercial and imperial hegemony in the Victorian era. (Royal Naval Museum, Portsmouth)

INTRODUCTION

The campaign of Trafalgar constituted only a short period in the naval conflict between Britain and France that had begun in 1793 and ended in 1815. It was, however, the most decisive, demonstrating not only Britain's naval power, but her significance as a major participant in a war waged on a scale that had not been seen before and which was not to be surpassed until the First World War. Within that campaign, the battle of Trafalgar itself stands as one of history's greatest naval encounters and the last great battle between wooden navies. In the course of a few hours Nelson eliminated forever the threat of a French invasion, and made Britain secure at sea for the next hundred years. It was a victory marred only by his death, although the fact that Nelson's demise coincided with his crowning achievement made possible his legendary status which persists to this day.

ORIGINS OF THE CAMPAIGN

Nelson's reputation was built as much on his character as on his victories at the Nile, Copenhagen and Trafalgar. By the time of his death at the age of 47 he had been at sea for a total of more than two decades. While it is true that his career was initially assisted by family connections, his extraordinary abilities, sheer determination and personal bravery propelled him from promotion to promotion.

Nelson was a simple man from a simple background, although he was by no means saintly in private or public life. He was openly unfaithful to his wife, he was vain, he questioned and even defied his superiors, and he was driven by self-promotion. He was, however, a consummate sailor and commander who never lost sight of his duty to his sovereign and country, and never doubted his ability to succeed in command, whether of a battery of guns or an entire fleet. He not only followed in the footsteps of Drake, Anson and others, but surpassed them all, developing tactics which were innovative yet founded on his own and other commanders' experiences. He displayed special concern for the welfare of his men, who repaid him with both admiration and devotion. He was almost universally admired and respected by his captains. George Duff of the *Mars* expressed a sentiment in a letter to his wife that was broadly representative: 'He is so good and pleasant a man, that we all wish to do what he likes, without any kind of orders.' Grown men wept when they learned of his death. Nelson distinguished himself not only from his contemporaries, but from all other naval commanders before or since.

By the time of Trafalgar, Napoleon had only been Emperor of France for a year. With the exception of a year of tenuous peace from 1802–03,

the great Globe itself, and all which it inherit, is too small to satisfy such insatiable appetite

Pitt and Napoleon carve up the world between them. Contemporary caricatures like these may have exaggerated their subjects, but the underlying message here is accurate: while Britain commanded the seas and expanded her overseas empire, France held sway over the European Continent. (Royal Naval Museum, Portsmouth)

the British and French had been at war since 1793, when the Revolutionaries extended their conflict against the Continental monarchies of Austria and Prussia to Britain. Britain not only opposed the principles being spread by force of arms by the Revolution, but would not countenance French domination of the European continent, above all the occupation of the Low Countries, which could serve as a springboard for an invasion of Britain. It was natural for an island nation of limited population and resources to support the needs of her navy over her army, but so long as the Continental powers failed to formulate a coherent strategy which brought together overwhelmingly superior forces on land, the threat of French power remained constant. So long as France continued to maintain a sizeable fleet, a landing on the English coast remained a distinct possibility.

While Britain's focus was on her navy, she had nevertheless provided handsome loans and subsidies to the Continental powers in the coalitions which her diplomacy and overseas trade largely created, but her own military contributions were confined to small, limited operations including one to Flanders in 1793, another to Toulon in the same year, various operations in the West Indies, and another to North Holland in 1799. Only the campaign of 1801 in Egypt proved a real success, but while it finally sealed the fate of Bonaparte's dream of an eastern empire, it had little impact on events in Europe, where the French had destroyed the First Coalition (1793–95) and then the Second (1798–1802), first by knocking Austria out of the war in 1801 and then making peace with Britain and Spain in 1802.

Yet if the French were clearly masters on land, the same certainly could not be said of them at sea, where they had suffered several major defeats, particularly at the hands of Nelson, who had destroyed the French Mediterranean fleet off the coast of Egypt in 1798. Nor were France's maritime allies safe: the Spanish and Dutch, allies of the French, were defeated at St Vincent and Camperdown, respectively, in 1797. British naval power extended into the Baltic when Sir Hyde Parker

William Pitt addressing the House of Commons on 1 February 1793, the first day of the war with Revolutionary France. In this, one of the greatest speeches ever delivered before Parliament, the Prime Minister declared: 'England will never consent that France shall arrogate the power of annulling at her pleasure, and under the pretence of a pretended natural right, of which she makes herself the only judge, the political system of Europe, established by solemn treaties and guaranteed by the consent of all the powers.' (National Portrait Gallery, London)

and Nelson quashed the League of Armed Neutrality with the virtual destruction of the Danish fleet at Copenhagen in 1801.

Such victories were significant not only for the protection of Britain's maritime trade, but also for her own security against invasion – in the summer of 1801 Napoleon renewed his plans for such operations. The French attempt at a landing in Ireland had failed in 1796–97, but the scheme had never been entirely shelved, not least because the Irish Rebellion in 1798 continued to give the French hope that Britain would be distracted by internal matters and a friendly Irish population might still make a landing practical.

Replacing William Pitt's ministry in 1801, Henry Addington opened negotiations for a preliminary peace with France and signed the Peace of Amiens in February 1802. By this agreement Britain returned all her colonial conquests taken from France, Spain and Holland except Spanish Trinidad and Dutch Ceylon (Sri Lanka). Addington recognized France's annexation of Savoy, control of the Cisalpine Republic (in northern Italy) and French occupation of Holland (United Provinces). But when Addington failed to stipulate the renewal of commercial relations with France, Napoleon was free to close French ports and colonies to British merchants at his discretion. In short, Amiens proved much more advantageous to France than to Britain. Technically speaking, Britain could not be a party to the guarantees France had provided to Austria at Lunéville in March 1801 by which French recognition of, and non-interference in, the Dutch, Swiss and Ligurian (northern Italian) Republics, had been guaranteed.

If Addington was perhaps too lenient in his settlement with France, at least he understood that Amiens constituted little more than an uneasy truce signed under conditions of stalemate and war weariness. The peace, in fact, lasted little more than a year. In the interim, Napoleon appointed himself president of the Cisalpine Republic, refused to withdraw his troops from Holland, intervened in internal Swiss affairs and banned British trade from markets in those parts of the Continent under French control. Britain, in turn, demanded the

Portsmouth dockyard. The majority of Royal Navy warships were constructed at the dockyards of Portsmouth, Plymouth, Chatham, Woolwich, Deptford and Sheerness, all of which also contained victualling yards, hospitals, Marine barracks and repair facilities. (Royal Naval Museum, Portsmouth)

Deptford shipyard on the Thames. One of several facilities run by the Navy Board, such yards constituted the largest industrial enterprises of their day anywhere in the world. Deptford had five slips for the construction of warships and was capable of building at least one first rate at a time. (Royal Naval Museum, Portsmouth)

immediate withdrawal of French forces from Holland, and objected to French interference in Switzerland and Italy.

Citing the need to strengthen her position in the Mediterranean as a counterweight to French expansion on the Continent, Britain refused to withdraw her troops from Malta, though this constituted a direct violation of Amiens. Malta was of particular strategic importance: it had been a landing point for Napoleon on his expedition to Egypt in 1798 and remained a potential springboard for future French operations in the central and eastern Mediterranean, which might include southern Italy, Greece or Egypt. So long as Malta remained in British hands, such places could receive British protection. By the spring of 1803 the French remained in Holland and Switzerland and the British continued to hold Malta. War therefore resumed on 18 May.

Britain stood alone against the threat of invasion, a threat which had its origins in Napoleon's original plans of the spring and summer of 1801, when he had ordered the assembly of ships and men at Boulogne on the north-west coast of France. Soon after his return from the Baltic, Nelson was sent in command of a force to attack and capture the enemy vessels at anchor in Boulogne. His foray of 15 August failed badly; French forces remained in place, the flotilla continued to grow and the likelihood of invasion increased. The Peace of Amiens forestalled this threat.

When war resumed, Addington soon put in train legislation to meet the renewed threat of invasion. His Army Reserve Acts of 1802 and 1803 raised 30,000 men, over half of whom transferred to the regular army. The Volunteers Act raised a staggering 300,000 men in England and 70,000 in Ireland. While it took many months to train men in such numbers, by 1804 they had established effective units capable of assisting in the nation's defence. The 'property tax' brought in one shilling in the pound on incomes over £150. Addington thus put Britain's war footing on a respectable level, even before Pitt resumed office in May.

It was, ironically, the Royal Navy which was least prepared for conflict at precisely the moment when the nation absolutely depended on it. Lord St Vincent, the First Lord of the Admiralty, had, during the peace, sold off large quantities of naval supplies such as surplus hemp, discharged 1,100 men from the dockyards and drastically reduced the number of ships in commission. With Napoleon's ambitious naval programme revived and the potential that France could unite her fleets with those of potential allies – particularly Spain – Britain could not afford to be complacent. Large amounts of timber were purchased and orders were placed for the construction of ships of the line. Existing vessels were re-commissioned, crews were recruited, squadrons weighed anchor and the naval blockade of French ports was immediately re-imposed.

Yet a defensive strategy was not enough. If Britain was to remove the threat of invasion, she would have to confront and destroy a substantial portion of the French fleet in open battle.

CHRONOLOGY

1803

16 May Nelson appointed Commander-in-Chief of the Mediterranean Fleet.

18 May Britain declares war on France, formally opening the Napoleonic Wars.

23 May Berthier, French Minister of War, announces first tentative plans for invasion camps along the Channel coast.

10 Sept Napoleon prepares project for initial invasion force of 114,000 men and 7,000 horses.

19 Oct Secret Franco-Spanish military alliance concluded.

1804

Jan 70,000 French troops encamped near Boulogne.

July Napoleon reviews the army and navy at Boulogne.

5 Oct Moore seizes Spanish treasure ships off Cadiz.

12 Dec Spain declares war on Britain.

1805

18 Jan Villeneuve makes abortive attempt to leave Toulon.

30 March Villeneuve sails from Toulon for Martinique.

4 April Nelson learns of Villeneuve's escape from Toulon.

10 April Villeneuve, with Gravina's squadron, sails from Cadiz for Martinique.

11 April Britain and Russia conclude an alliance against France.

12 May Nelson leaves Portuguese waters for the West Indies, in pursuit of the Combined Fleet.

16 May Villeneuve's fleet reaches Fort de France, Martinique.

June Collingwood ordered south, ultimately to Cadiz.

4 June Nelson arrives at Carlisle Bay, Barbados.

7 June Villeneuve learns of Nelson's arrival in the West Indies.

16 June Nelson learns of Villeneuve's departure for Europe.

17 July Allemand's squadron escapes from Rochefort.

22 July Calder's force clashes indecisively with the Combined Fleet off Ferrol.

27 July Villeneuve puts into Vigo Bay, on the north-west coast of Spain.

31 July Villeneuve leaves Vigo for Ferrol, arriving two days later.

9 Aug Austria formally joins Britain and Russia in the Third Coalition against France.

11 Aug Combined Fleet sails south for Cadiz.

18 Aug Nelson reaches Portsmouth and begins short stay in Britain.

26 Aug *Grande Armée* at Boulogne breaks camp and marches for the Rhine.

15 Sept Nelson sails from Portsmouth to join Collingwood's force off Cadiz.

28 Sept Nelson assumes command of the Mediterranean Fleet.

19 Oct First French ships leave Cadiz; Nelson orders pursuit.

20 Oct Remainder of Combined Fleet leaves Cadiz.

21 Oct Battle of Trafalgar.

4 Nov Strachan captures Dumanoir's four ships off Cape Ortegal, off north-west Spanish coast.

6 Nov News of Trafalgar reaches London.

2 Dec Battle of Austerlitz: Napoleon decisively defeats Austro-Russian army in Moravia; Third Coalition collapses.

4 Dec HMS *Victory* arrives in England bearing Nelson's body.

1806

9 Jan Nelson's state funeral in St Paul's Cathedral.

OPPOSING COMMANDERS

Lord Nelson. No naval commander before or since has possessed the sort of charismatic appeal, tactical genius, personal bravery and instinct for duty which together make Nelson history's greatest admiral. Trafalgar secured his apotheosis. (Royal Naval Museum, Portsmouth)

BRITISH COMMANDERS

The greatest sailor of his day and perhaps of any era, Vice-Admiral Horatio Nelson was born in Burnham Thorpe, Norfolk, in 1758, the fifth of 11 children to the Reverend Edmund Nelson and his wife, Catherine. He entered the Royal Navy at the age of 12 through the patronage provided by his maternal uncle, Captain Maurice Suckling, who became Comptroller of the Navy shortly after Nelson joined the service. Young Nelson went aboard the *Raisonnable* in 1771, having been sent to the West Indies in a merchant vessel. He returned to England after a year to join the *Triumph* before, in 1773, being chosen to assist in an expedition to the Arctic. On his return later the same year he was sent in the *Seahorse* to the East Indies for a short time, before being invalided home in 1776 and transferred to the *Worcester* as acting lieutenant. After six months his rank was confirmed and he returned to the West Indies aboard the frigate *Lowestoft*.

Through family connections Nelson received command of the brigantine *Badger* in December 1778, and was ordered to protect British trade along the Mosquito Coast (Honduras) from American privateers. In June 1779 he was promoted to post-captain of the *Hinchinbrook* before, at the beginning of the following year, serving in the expedition against Fort San Juan from which he was withdrawn after falling dangerously ill from fever. He was evacuated to Jamaica and placed in

Nelson boarding the *San Josef* at the battle of St Vincent, 14 February 1797. Always leading from the front and exposing himself to danger whatever the risks, Nelson established a reputation for courage bordering on recklessness, a feature with immense appeal in an age which adored its heroes. (Alfred and Roland Umhey Collection)

command of the *Janus*, although his sickness prevented him from carrying out his duties and he was invalided home.

After convalescing at Bath, Nelson went aboard the *Albermarle* and sailed to Canada, arriving in July 1782. From Halifax he sailed to the West Indies in May 1783 under Admiral Hood, before being sent home for six months. In March 1784, in command of the *Boreas*, Nelson sailed to the West Indies where he tried to put a stop to the illegal trade conducted by American merchants selling goods to British colonies. While on the island of Nevis he met Frances Nisbet, a widow, whom he married in March 1787. The couple returned to England where Nelson went on half pay for the next five years.

In January 1793, just as war broke out with France, Nelson was given command of the *Agamemnon* and directed to sail to the Mediterranean to join Lord Hood's fleet. Nelson fought on Corsica, where he lost the sight of his right eye at Calvi in July 1794, and became a commodore in April 1796. He came into prominence ten months later when he fought with distinction at the battle of St Vincent against the Spanish. He was knighted and promoted to rear-admiral. In July 1797 he led an unsuccessful attack on Santa Cruz, Tenerife, in which he was severely wounded in the right arm by grapeshot. Nelson's arm was amputated and he was sent home, where he had an audience with King George III and received a pension. Despite his fear that his incapacity would prevent him from further service, Nelson raised his flag in the *Vanguard* in April 1798, and rejoined the Mediterranean Fleet.

Although his principal mission was to watch the Toulon fleet, a gale blew him off station and when he was finally able to make repairs, the French had left port. Using intelligence that suggested that Bonaparte was bound for Egypt, Nelson went in pursuit, reaching Alexandria in June. The French were nowhere to be seen, but upon returning to the Egyptian coast after stopping for provisions at Syracuse, on 1 August, Nelson discovered Admiral Brueys' fleet anchored in Aboukir Bay. He surprised the enemy that evening, taking 13 enemy vessels and thus ruining Bonaparte's plans to conquer Egypt permanently and to march overland to India.

On reaching Naples after the battle he was given a hero's welcome and heaped with honours and rewards, including a peerage as Baron

Battle of Copenhagen, 2 April 1801. The second of Nelson's triumvirate of great naval successes, this battle was not fought in the open sea, but by a British fleet engaging its Danish counterpart while the latter lay anchored in harbour and protected by forts and floating batteries. (Royal Naval Museum, Portsmouth)

Nelson of the Nile and Burnham Thorpe. In the course of his stay in Naples, at the house of the British Ambassador, Sir William Hamilton, Nelson met Emma, Lady Hamilton, with whom a romance developed. Nelson was soon recalled, partly because of the embarrassment being caused by his affair with Lady Hamilton, but also as a result of the revolutionary movement then brewing in the Kingdom of Naples that had forced the king and queen to transfer their court to Sicily.

Nelson returned home in 1800 and separated from his wife. In the same year he was promoted to vice-admiral and sent to Yarmouth where he joined the fleet under Admiral Sir Hyde Parker as second-in-command of an expedition to the Baltic. Russia, Sweden, Denmark and Prussia had formed the League of Armed Neutrality in order to oppose trade restrictions Britain had imposed on these neutral states. Nelson led the attack against the anchored Danish fleet at Copenhagen in 1801, destroying much of it and forcing Denmark out of the League. He was made a viscount and succeeded Parker as commander-in-chief in the Baltic. Returning to Yarmouth, Nelson was then appointed to command a flotilla designed to defend the south coast of England from French invasion. In this capacity he took part in an abortive attack against the harbour at Boulogne.

When peace was restored with France by the Treaty of Amiens in 1802, Nelson returned home, purchased a house at Merton in Surrey and moved in, though he spent a considerable time at the Hamiltons' home in London, carrying on his affair with Emma. After Sir William's death in April, Nelson and Emma lived together at Merton, unmarried. Peace with France lasted little more than a year, however, and when war resumed in May 1804 Nelson was given command of the Mediterranean Fleet, his purpose to observe the enemy naval force at Toulon and engage it if it emerged from port. A chance to confront it finally arrived in the spring of 1805 when Villeneuve escaped from Toulon, in accordance with Napoleon's plan to unite his various squadrons in a bid to gain control of the Channel.

Vice-Admiral Cuthbert Collingwood (1748–1810). He served under Sir Robert Calder while blockading Cadiz before Nelson appointed him second-in-command of the Mediterranean fleet in September 1805. (Royal Naval Museum, Portsmouth)

Vice-Admiral Cuthbert Collingwood was Nelson's second-in-command at Trafalgar. Born in Newcastle in 1750, Collingwood first volunteered to serve aboard the frigate *Shannon* at the age of 11. In 1775, during the War of American Independence, he was promoted to lieutenant and he met Nelson the following year while both were serving on the *Lowestoft*. In the same year Collingwood was tried by court martial for disobedience and neglect of duty. On being acquitted of all charges, he was made, as a result of Nelson's promotion to post rank, commander of the *Badger*. He served in the West Indies on a number of occasions and fought at the battle of the Glorious First of June in 1794. The following year he was assigned to the Mediterranean Fleet. On promotion to rear-admiral in 1799, Collingwood hoisted his flag in the *Triumph* in the Channel Fleet. In 1804 he was promoted to vice-admiral, and the following year he was placed in command of a squadron dispatched to reinforce Nelson's fleet in the Mediterranean.

Captain the Hon. Henry Blackwood (1770–1832), a close friend of Nelson's, was 35 at Trafalgar and had served in the navy since the age of 11, nearly always aboard frigates, where he earned for himself an excellent reputation for sailing faster than his colleagues. He came to the fore when, in a celebrated ship-to-ship action off Malta in 1802, he intercepted and engaged the *Guillaume Tell*, 80, with his own diminutive *Penelope*, 32. The enemy ship of the line happened to be the flagship of Admiral Denis Decrès, who would shortly thereafter become Minister of the Navy. Undaunted neither by circumstances – the action was fought at night and in a gale – nor by the disparity of strength between his own vessel and that of his opponent, Blackwood maintained the fight until morning, when the crippled *Guillaume Tell* was finally captured by British ships of the line arriving at the scene. In October 1805, in command of the frigate *Euryalus*, Blackwood commanded the inshore squadron off Cadiz, signalling Nelson when the Combined Fleet emerged from the harbour.

Sir William Cornwallis (1744–1819), the fourth son of Charles, fifteenth Lord and First Earl Cornwallis, one of the unsung heroes of the Trafalgar campaign, was made a lieutenant in 1761 and captain in 1766. In the course of his long naval career he served in the Channel, the Mediterranean, the Atlantic, the Caribbean, and off the African coast, during which time he fought in numerous actions against the French. Cornwallis met Nelson in the West Indies in the 1780s and fought with distinction under Admiral Sir Samuel Hood at the Battle of St Kitts in 1782. He was made Commander-in-Chief of the East Indies station in 1788, promoted to rear-admiral on the first day of the war against France (1 February 1793), and made vice-admiral the following year. In February 1796 he was appointed Commander-in-Chief in the West Indies, but was recalled due to ill health. Promoted to full admiral in February 1799, two years later he succeeded Lord St Vincent in command of the Channel Fleet until peace was concluded in March 1802. When war resumed in May 1803, Cornwallis took up the same post, which entailed the arduous task of maintaining the blockade of Brest. This he conducted with great skill while lying off Ushant; his patience, over two years, in keeping the French in port played a vital, though unfairly forgotten, part in the campaign.

Vice-Admiral Pierre Villeneuve (1763–1806). Commander of the Toulon fleet in 1804, he thereafter led the Combined (Franco-Spanish) fleet at Trafalgar, where he was captured. Granted parole, he attended Nelson's funeral and then returned to France, where he was blamed for the defeat and died in prison in mysterious circumstances. (PH 85905: 'L'Amiral Villeneuve, commandant en chef des escadres alliées à Trafalgar.' © Musée national de la marine, Paris)

Admiral Federico Carlos Gravina (1758–1806). Second-in-command of the Combined Fleet at Trafalgar, where he was mortally wounded. (Alfred and Roland Umhey Collection)

FRENCH COMMANDERS

Vice-Admiral Pierre Charles Jean Baptiste Silvestre Villeneuve (1763–1806) commanded the French fleet at Trafalgar, having succeeded Admiral La Touche-Treville in August 1804. Napoleon, however, had lost confidence in Villeneuve, and though Admiral Rosily was appointed in his stead, he was not yet in command when the British and Combined Fleets met on 21 October. Of an aristocratic family from Provençal, Villeneuve had nevertheless served successive revolutionary governments under whom he earned rapid promotion, reaching the rank of rear-admiral by the age of 33. He had served under the distinguished Admiral Suffren during the War of American Independence and had fought Nelson at the battle of the Nile in 1798. He had little confidence in his own abilities and came into conflict with his Spanish allies over strategy. Collingwood described him as 'a well-bred man and, I believe, a very good officer; he has nothing in his manner of the offensive vapouring and boasting which we, perhaps too often, attribute to Frenchmen.' Villeneuve's second-in-command, Rear-Admiral P. R. Dumanoir Le Pelley, 35 at the time of Trafalgar, had also served the Revolution in spite of his aristocratic background. His conduct at Trafalgar was to play an important role in the outcome of the battle.

SPANISH COMMANDERS

Admiral Don Federico Gravina (1758–1806), second-in-command at Trafalgar, was born in Palermo to an old Sicilian family. Close links with the royal family enabled him to accompany King Charles (Carlos) III to Spain, where Gravina entered the Spanish Navy. He would distinguish himself several times in actions at sea. In 1788, aged 32, he went to Constantinople to study astronomy and later studied the Royal Navy in Britain at the behest of the Spanish government. He fought at Toulon against the French revolutionaries in 1793, then in the defence of Rosas, and later at Cadiz against the British.

In 1801 Gravina was sent to the Spanish part of the island of San Domingo in the West Indies to co-operate with the French Navy against the British. When Napoleon crowned himself Emperor three years later, Gravina was dispatched to Paris as ambassador from Spain and as the Spanish royal family's representative at the coronation in Nôtre Dame Cathedral.

Gravina was senior to Villeneuve in age, and at 49 he would not conceal the reluctance he felt in serving under his French ally, whom he disliked, a circumstance which left the two senior Allied commanders unable to co-operate effectively during the campaign. Gravina's second-in-command was Vice-Admiral Don Ignatius Maria de Alava (1750–1817), aged 52.

OPPOSING NAVIES

THE ROYAL NAVY

At the beginning of 1803 Britain had only 32 line of battle ships in commission. The pace of building and re-fitting increased rapidly, however, and by June there were 60 ships ready for sea, the total rising by the end of the year to 75 ships of the line and 320 other vessels, of which 114 were frigates. The necessities of war led to rapid expansion of the fleet. By the end of 1804 there were 83 ships of the line in commission and the number of smaller vessels reached 425, with 109,000 men in all capacities at home and at sea throughout the world, though principally in European and West Indian waters. Command in January 1805 was divided as follows: Admiral Cornwallis in the Channel, Admiral Lord Keith in the North Sea, and Vice-Admiral Viscount Nelson in the Mediterranean. Command in the West Indies was divided between Sir John Duckworth in Jamaica and Rear-Admiral Sir Alexander Cochrane in the Leeward Islands. Finally, Rear-Admirals Sir Edward Pellew and Sir Thomas Troubridge shared joint command in the remote East Indies.

Such men, and the many ships' captains under them, were first-rate commanders, a fact confirmed by an exchange between Lord Barham, the First Lord of the Admiralty, and Nelson, while the admiral was back in England during a brief stay in the summer of 1805 and preparing to put to sea. Barham handed him a list of the Navy's officers, asking him

HMS *Victory*. A classic three-decker ship of the line, she was launched in 1765, making her a veteran of 40 years' service by the time of Trafalgar, when her ship's company numbered 820, over 100 of whom were foreigners. She was constructed of 300,000 cubic feet of timber (c.6,000 oak trees), she used 26 miles of hemp for her standing and running rigging, and her sails required over 6,500 square yards of canvas. She cost a staggering £63,176 (over £50 million in today's terms). (Royal Naval Museum, Portsmouth)

Boarding. Fighting at close quarters involved the use of a host of weapons, including cutlasses, pistols, pikes, boarding axes, bayonets and musket butts. Marines played an important part in repelling boarders, and their fire supplemented the efforts of the gun crews who employed grapeshot as an anti-personnel measure. (National Maritime Museum, Greenwich: Neg x164)

A British gun crew. In addition to possessing superior skills in seamanship, Royal Navy crews were highly trained in the handling of ships' guns, proficiency at which could only be acquired after extensive drill. (Royal Naval Museum, Portsmouth)

to choose the men he wished to command. Returning the list, Nelson replied, 'Choose yourself, my Lord. The same spirit actuates the whole profession; you cannot choose wrong.'

The Royal Navy enjoyed a number of advantages over their adversaries, including superior training, tactics, morale and seamanship. Only in the field of ship design could the British be said to be inferior to their contemporaries. In technology – specifically in gunnery – the British possessed an advantage, using flintlocks instead of slow-matches, although the latter they kept burning in case their flintlocks misfired. A flintlock fired a gun within an instant, so that a gunner could discharge his weapon on the ship's roll at the moment when he was satisfied with the elevation of his gun.

British tactics emphasized the offensive. The Royal Navy almost exclusively employed round shot and aimed at their enemy's hull with the express intention of battering him into submission. Firing round shot at the side of an enemy ship might disable or kill the gunners and render their guns unserviceable, but it rarely crippled the ship so badly that it could not be salvaged after the battle. The hull also offered a bigger target than the rigging, and when judging the elevation became difficult in heavy seas, the gunner was much more likely to hit the hull. Even when a shot missed, if it travelled too high it might still damage the rigging. A financial incentive also dictated British tactics. In a profession where conditions were harsh and pay was low, prize money offered a great attraction. British crews always sought to capture an enemy vessel with its masts and rigging largely undamaged, so that once taken, the ship could be sailed back to England and brought into the service of the Royal Navy in exchange for payment, or prize money from the Admiralty.

Many factors contributed to the consistent success enjoyed by the Royal Navy over her adversaries: from the superior strategy formulated by the Admiralty at the top, to the seamanship, discipline, gunnery and fighting spirit of the crews at the bottom.

THE FRENCH NAVY

Napoleon did not expect war to be resumed so soon. In May 1803 he had only 47 ships of the line ready for service, with another 19 under construction or on order. Those afloat were dispersed amongst numerous harbours: 21 line of battle ships in Brest; 12 in Toulon; and nine en route for Europe from San Domingo, eventually to arrive in Rochefort, Ferrol and Cadiz. With these ships so scattered, the crews poorly trained and their numbers inferior to those of the British, no fleet operations of any significance could be attempted, and thus the navy was told to complete the ships already under construction as quickly as possible. In the meantime, apart from privateering, Napoleon struck at Britain by the only means available to him: he invaded the north German state of Hanover (the patrimony of George III), and resumed his plans for an amphibious landing on the south coast of England.

The Peace of Amiens had in fact provided Napoleon time to resurrect his plans to invade England. From March 1803 the Minister of the Navy, Denis Decrès, had begun work on 150 shallow draught landing craft, with orders for over 1,000 more issued in May. In July he issued orders for the purchase and construction of more than 2,400 additional vessels. While this impressive naval building programme was under way, Napoleon began concentrating large numbers of troops along the Channel coasts and established the headquarters of his invasion force at Boulogne. Once the French Navy could provide a proper escort for these troops in their otherwise extremely vulnerable landing craft, Napoleon would stand a realistic chance of success.

By the beginning of 1805 his prospects were improving, for the French Navy then consisted of 56 ships of the line ready for sea and another 15 in various phases of construction. All told, the French and Spanish (allies as of December 1804) could deploy 102 line of battle ships at a time when the British had only 83 in commission. Having said this, practically every French and Spanish squadron remained under close British blockade until the spring of 1805, and with their ships

French sailor. The French Navy recruited men largely through a system of conscription dating back more than a century by the time of Trafalgar. A man was registered by the state, and called up when required. Seamen were categorized into four classes: unmarried men, widowers without children, married men without children and fathers of families. (Alfred and Roland Umhey Collection)

The French ship *Incorruptible*. If French crews did not possess the standard of seamanship and gunnery skills of their British counterparts, their bravery was seldom in question and the craftsmanship and design of their vessels were widely regarded as superior to that of the Royal Navy. (National Maritime Museum, Greenwich: Neg A652)

Spanish sailor. Always in critically short supply, usually conscripted and chronically ill-trained, the Spanish crews were largely landsmen, with only a smattering of genuine sailors amongst them, and only a few of these with experience of sailing beyond the Spanish coastline. (Alfred and Roland Umhey Collection)

confined to port the seamen could not be properly drilled, causing deterioration in morale and standards of shiphandling and gunnery.

If the ordinary seamen left much to be desired, so did the officer corps, which had been denuded by the reforms and chaos of the Revolution. These problems were compounded by Napoleon's lack of confidence in his admirals in particular, and in his fleets in general. The Emperor took an extremely keen interest in his army and in the conduct of land warfare, but his military genius did not extend to an understanding of strategy and tactics at sea. Unsurprisingly, a much greater proportion of the nation's resources were expended on Napoleon's favoured arm of the fighting services. Morale within the navy naturally suffered as a result.

Both technically and tactically, the French laboured under disadvantages. Despite the existence of the superior flintlock method of discharging small arms and artillery, the French continued to employ slow-matches to fire their naval guns. Slow-matches fired only after an unpredictable delay, which meant that as the ship rolled, the elevation – and therefore the range – could not be estimated with much accuracy. Aiming from a rolling ship was the most difficult aspect of naval gunnery.

Tactically, French training emphasized the defensive, with crews preferring to aim at an enemy's rigging. For this they chose ammunition suited to the task: bar and chain shot, specifically designed to shred sails and cut spars and ropes. By shooting at the rigging the French hoped to disable and, preferably, dismast their enemy, so denying him motive power and preventing him from pursuit or escape. By firing at the rigging the French also suffered from the disadvantage of sometimes missing their target altogether, for a shot aimed too high simply flew over the masts, while a shot fired too low – even if it were bar or chain shot which could not penetrate the hull – normally bounced harmlessly off the ship's side. Nor would they accrue any (albeit slight) benefit from the effect of ricochet off the water which was sometimes achieved by round shot.

ORDERS OF BATTLE

British Fleet at Trafalgar, 21 October 1805

Commander-in-Chief: Vice-Admiral Lord Nelson, KB

Total fleet strength:
27 ships of the line (c.17,000 officers and men; 2,148 guns)
four frigates and two auxiliaries

Weather Column

Ships	Guns	Killed	Wounded	Commander
Victory	100	57	102	Vice-Adm Viscount Nelson, KB
				Capt Thomas Hardy
Téméraire	98	47	76	Capt Eliab Harvey
Neptune	98	10	34	Capt Thomas Fremantle
Conqueror	74	3	9	Capt Israel Pellew
Agamemnon	64	2	8	Capt Sir Edward Berry
Britannia	100	10	40	Rear-Adm the Earl of Northesk; Capt Charles Bullen
Leviathan	74	4	22	Capt Henry Bayntun
Ajax	74	2	9	Lt John Pilfold (acting in the absence of Capt William Brown)
Orion	74	1	23	Capt Edward Codrington
Minotaur	74	3	20	Capt Charles Mansfield
Africa	64	18	44	Capt Henry Digby
Spartiate	74	3	20	Capt Sir Francis Laforey, Bt
Prince*	98	0	0	Capt Richard Grindall

*Often listed as belonging to the lee division, yet she sailed into battle with the weather division.

Lee Column

Ships	Guns	Killed	Wounded	Commander
Mars	74	29	69	Capt George Duff
Royal Sovereign	100	47	94	Vice-Admiral Cuthbert Collingwood; Capt Edward Rotheram
Tonnant	80	26	50	Capt Charles Tyler
Belleisle	74	33	93	Capt William Hargood
Bellerophon	74	27	123	Capt John Cooke
Colossus	74	40	160	Capt James Nicoll Morris
Achille	74	13	59	Capt Richard King
Polyphemus	64	2	4	Capt Robert Redmill
Revenge	74	28	51	Capt Robert Moorsom
Swiftsure	74	9	8	Capt William Rutherford
Defence	74	7	29	Capt George Hope
Thunderer	74	4	12	Lt John Stockham (acting in the absence of Capt William Lechmere)
Defiance	74	17	53	Capt Philip Durham
Dreadnought	98	7	26	Capt John Conn

Other vessels

Frigates

Ships	Guns	Killed	Wounded	Commander
Euryalus	36	0	0	Capt the Hon. Henry Blackwood
Naiad	38	0	0	Capt Thomas Dundas
Phoebe	36	0	0	Capt the Hon. Thomas Bladen Capel
Sirius	36	0	0	Capt William Prowse

Schooners

Pickle	10	0	0	Lt John Lapenotière

Cutters

Entreprenante	8	0	0	Lt Robert Young

Spanish sea-soldier. Like their allies, the Spanish failed to meet the insatiable manpower needs of their navy, as a consequence of which they sought to bolster their crews with soldiers. Unaccustomed to life – much less combat – at sea, they proved something of a liability, being practically useless except as musketeers. (Alfred and Roland Umhey Collection)

Combined (Franco-Spanish) Fleet at Trafalgar, 21 October 1805

Commander-in-Chief:
Vice-Admiral Pierre Charles Jean Baptiste Silvestre Villeneuve

Fleet strength:
33 ships of the line (c.30,000 officers and men; 2,632 guns)
five frigates and two auxiliaries

Van squadron

Ship	Guns	Commander	Killed	Wounded	Fate
San Justo (Sp)	74	Capt Don Miguel Gastón	0	7	Escaped to Cadiz.
Indomptable (Fr)	80	Capt Jean-Joseph Hubert	unknown		Escaped; sortied 23 Oct; went ashore and wrecked, 24 Oct.
Santa Ana (Sp)	112	Vice-Adm Don Ignatius Maria de Alava; Capt Don José Gardoquí	97	141	Captured by Royal Sovereign; retaken during sortie, 23 Oct; returned to Cadiz.
Fougueux (Fr)	74	Capt Louis-Alexis Beaudouin	300 killed and wounded		Captured by Téméraire; ran ashore and wrecked, 22 Oct.
Monarca (Sp)	74	Capt Don Teodoro Argumosa	101	154	Captured by Bellerophon; ran ashore and wrecked, 25 Oct.
Pluton (Fr)	74	Commodore Julien Cosmao-Kerjulien	c.300 casualties		Escaped to Cadiz; sortied 23 Oct.

Centre Squadron

Ship	Guns	Commander	Killed	Wounded	Fate
San Agustín (Sp)	74	Capt Don Felipe Xado Cagigal	184	201	Captured by Leviathan; set on fire, 30 Oct.
Héros (Fr)	74	Capt Jean-Baptiste Poulain	12	24	Escaped to Cadiz with damaged rigging and rudder.
Santísima Trinidad (Sp)	140	Rear-Adm Don Hidalgo Cisneros; Commodore Don Francisco de Uriarte	216	116	Captured by Prince; dismasted; foundered and sank, 24 Oct.
Bucentaure (Fr)	80	Vice-Adm Pierre Villeneuve; Capt Jean-Jacques Magendie	197	85	Captured by Conqueror; dismasted; ran ashore and wrecked, 23 Oct.
Neptune (Fr)	84	Commodore Esprit-Tranquille Maistral	15	39	Escaped to Cadiz; sortied 23 Oct.
San Leandro (Sp)	64	Capt Don José Quevedo	8	22	Escaped to Cadiz.
Redoutable (Fr)	74	Capt Jean-Jacques Lucas	474	70	Captured by Téméraire; dismasted; foundered and sank, 22 Oct.

Rear Squadron

Ship	Guns	Commander	Killed	Wounded	Fate
Neptuno (Sp)	80	Capt Don Cayetano Valdés	42	47	Captured by Minotaur; recaptured 23 Oct; wrecked; set on fire 31 Oct.
Scipion (Fr)	74	Capt Charles Bérenger	0	0	Escaped; captured by Strachan, 4 Nov.
Rayo (Sp)	100	Capt Don Enrique Macdonnell	4	14	Escaped to Cadiz; sortied 23 Oct; captured by Donegal; went ashore and wrecked; set on fire 31 Oct.
Formidable (Fr)	80	Rear-Adm Pierre Dumanoir Le Pelley; Capt Jean-Marie Lettelier	22	45	Escaped; captured by Strachan, 4 Nov.
Duguay-Trouin (Fr)	74	Capt Claude Touffet	12	24	Escaped; captured by Strachan, 4 Nov.
San Francisco de Asís (Sp)	74	Capt Don Luis de Flores	5	12	Escaped to Cadiz; sortied 23 Oct; went ashore and wrecked same day.
Mont-Blanc (Fr)	74	Capt Noel La Villegris	0	0	Escaped; captured by Strachan, 4 Nov.
Intrépide (Fr)	74	Capt Louis Infernet	306 killed and wounded		Captured by Orion; set on fire, 24 Oct.

Squadron of Observation

Ship	Guns	Commander	Killed	Wounded	Fate
Algésiras (Fr)	74	Rear-Adm Charles Magon de Médine; Cmdr Laurent Le Tourneur (acting on behalf of Capt Gabriel Auguste Brouard)	77	142	Captured by Tonnant; retaken from prize crew and returned to Cadiz.
Bahama (Sp)	74	Commodore Don Dionisio Alcalá Galiano	c.400 killed and wounded		Captured by Colossus; taken to Gibraltar and commissioned into Royal Navy.
Aigle (Fr)	74	Capt Pierre Gourrège	270 killed and wounded		Captured by Defiance; ran ashore and wrecked, 25 Oct.
Swiftsure (Fr)	74	Capt Charles-Eusèba L'Hôpitalier-Villemadrin	250 killed and wounded		Captured by Colossus; taken to Gibraltar and commissioned into Royal Navy.
Argonaute (Fr)	74	Capt Jacques Epron	55	132	Escaped to Cadiz with serious damage.
Montañes (Sp)	74	Capt Don Josef Alcedo	20	29	Escaped to Cadiz.
Argonauta (Sp)	80	Capt Don Antonio Pareja	100	203	Captured by Belleisle; scuttled, 30 Oct.
Berwick (Fr)	74	Capt Jean Filhol-Camas	250 killed and wounded; mostly drowned		Captured by Achille; ran ashore and wrecked, 27 Oct.
San Juan Nepomuceno (Sp)	74	Commodore Don Cosmé Churruca	300 killed and wounded		Captured by Dreadnought; taken to Gibraltar and commissioned into Royal Navy.
San Ildefonso (Sp)	74	Commodore Don José de Vargas	34	126	Captured by Defence; commissioned into Royal Navy.
Achille (Fr)	74	Capt Louis Denieport	Nearly entire crew made casualties		Caught fire in action against the Prince and blew up.
Principe de Asturias (Sp)	112	Adm Don Federico Carlos de Gravina; Rear-Adm Don Antonio Escaño; Capt Rafael de Hore	41	107	Escaped to Cadiz.

Other vessels (frigates and brigs)

Rhin (Fr)	40	Capt Chesneau
Hortense (Fr)	40	Capt La Marre La Meillerie
Cornélie (Fr)	40	Capt de Martinenq
Thémis (Fr)	40	Capt Jugan
Hermione (Fr)	40	Capt Mahe
Furet (Fr)	18	Lt Dumay
Argus (Fr)	16	Lt Taillard

Note on ships' names
Certain ships in both fleets bore similar or even identical names, either through coincidence or owing to the fact that they had been previously captured from an enemy and their original names retained. Thus, the two fleets contained the *Neptuno* (Sp), *Neptune* (Fr) and *Neptune* (Br), while the British and French each had an *Achille* and a *Swiftsure*, the French *Swiftsure* having been taken from the British in 1801. The French also had the *Berwick*, also originally British, while their opponents had the *Téméraire* and *Tonnant*, prizes taken from French.

Note on disposition of Allied squadrons
This order of battle represents that which Villeneuve commanded when his fleet left Cadiz. However, when he ordered his ships to reverse course just prior to battle, his squadrons assumed different positions.

THE SPANISH NAVY

By the Treaty of San Ildefonso (1796) Spain had been obliged to furnish France with 15 ships of the line and a contingent of troops. In 1803 Napoleon renewed this demand, offering Spain the alternative of declaring war on Britain, which of course would bring her entire navy into the balance. Initially, Spain agreed to supply the ships and men as before, but when London's repeated warnings to desist went unheeded, in October 1804 four British ships off Cadiz attacked an equal number of Spanish vessels carrying treasure worth over £1 million. Spain duly declared war in December. In a stroke, France now possessed a numerical advantage in ships over the Royal Navy.

At the beginning of 1805 the Spanish navy consisted of 31 ships of the line stationed at Ferrol on the north-west coast, Cadiz to the south near Gibraltar and Cartagena on the east coast in the Mediterranean. The quality of Spanish naval crews left much to be desired, a Spanish admiral noting the sailors' lack of initiative and reliance on the orders of their superiors:

> *Experience shows … that a Spaniard, working under a system which leans to formality and strict order being maintained in battle, has no feeling for mutual support, and goes into action with hesitation, preoccupied with the anxiety of seeing or hearing the commander-in-chief's signals for such and such manoeuvres. Thus they can never make up their minds to seize any favourable opportunity that may present itself. They are fettered by the strict rule to keep station, which is enforced upon them …*

Spain had, indeed, been badly defeated at Cape St Vincent in 1797, but was not vanquished, and many of her men were willing and able to fight. Indeed, a number of British contemporaries remarked on Spanish bravery. William Robinson, a midshipman aboard the *Revenge* observed that at Trafalgar 'the Dons [Spanish] fought as well as the French … and if praise was due for seamanship and valour, they were well entitled to an equal share.'

The Spanish officer corps was of mixed quality, though unlike its French counterpart, it had not been affected by revolutionary upheaval. Some of Gravina's officers particularly distinguished themselves, such as Captain Don Cosmé Churruca of the *San Juan Nepomuceno*, whom one seaman described thus:

> *Our leader seemed to have infused his heroic spirit into the crew and soldiers, and the ship was handled and her broadsides delivered with wonderful promptitude and accuracy. Churruca directed battle with gloomy calmness. He saw to everything, settled everything, and the shot flew round him and over his head without his ever once even changing colour.*

OPPOSING PLANS

FRENCH PLANS

Napoleon realized by the end of the summer of 1804 that while his traditional emphasis on land operations had resulted in great territorial acquisitions for France in the campaigns of the 1790s, at sea Britain remained dominant. With French squadrons sitting idle, blockaded in every port, Britain stood between Napoleon and French hegemony over the Continent. Blessed with lucrative colonial goods and secure sea lanes, Britain could continue to finance any nation opposing Napoleonic rule with massive subsidies. These were made possible by a combination of levies on imported goods, domestic taxation and loans secured by Parliament. British control of the sea, moreover, left France unable to pursue any colonial ambitions, thus further reducing her ability to increase her revenue through maritime trade. Finally, and most importantly, without the protection afforded by a sizeable French battle fleet, the invasion flotilla assembling along the Channel coast could not possibly succeed.

In July 1804 Napoleon developed a grand strategy which, though it would undergo half a dozen variations until the spring of 1805, never changed in its basic objectives: that of breaking the blockades of his ports, combining as many French and Spanish ships of the line as possible and sailing them in overwhelming force to the English Channel. There, they would escort an invasion flotilla – the most formidable one assembled opposite the English coast since 1066 – which by the beginning of 1805 was intended to carry six army corps, totalling

French invasion craft. Napoleon's plan for a descent on the Kent coast never involved anything more complex than a flotilla (albeit a large one) of flat-bottomed boats, yet contemporary engravers took exceptional licence when depicting their version of the Emperor's capabilities. Genuine fear swept across Britain in 1803–05, giving rise to fantastic theories which claimed troops would arrive by balloon, by tunnel under the Channel, by windmill-propelled barges, and across a massive bridge spanning the 'ditch'. (National Maritime Museum, Greenwich: A5505)

160,000 men borne in over 2,000 craft. Success depended on control of the Channel – even if only for a few days – in order for the flotilla, otherwise defenceless against warships, to make the short crossing to the coast of Kent.

On 18 January 1805 Villeneuve put to sea from Toulon with 11 ships of the line and nine frigates to carry out a diversionary attack on Britain's West Indian possessions. Rear-Admiral Eduoard-Thomas de Burgues Missiessy (1756–1837) had escaped from Rochefort with orders to sail across the Atlantic and await Villeneuve's arrival. For the moment, Napoleon intended merely to concentrate naval forces in the West Indies in order to harass British possessions there rather than as a means of returning to Europe to execute his invasion plan. In any event, these ambitions were thwarted when Villeneuve found that with inexperienced crews and ships packed with troops and facing heavy weather, he had no choice but to put back into Toulon, into which they sailed on the 21st. Missiessy reached the West Indies as instructed, but without Villeneuve's force acting in tandem, the invasion plan was for a second time in abeyance.

With this plan thwarted, Napoleon quickly conceived another, which later became known as the 'Grand Design'. Developments in October 1804 had given Napoleon cause for optimism. As noted earlier, on the 5th of that month a British force had captured three Spanish frigates and sunk a fourth off Cadiz, in line with instructions from the Admiralty to prevent the landing of silver from the New World destined for French coffers. When Spain declared war on Britain on 12 December, she put at Napoleon's disposal nine ships of the line at Ferrol, six at Cartagena, and 16 at Cadiz. The Spanish immediately prepared these squadrons for readiness at sea, to be led by Admiral Gravina. With Spain now on his side and eagerly preparing for war, Napoleon no longer had need for elaborate diversions, but could pursue his ultimate objective directly.

The plan drawn up was not complex, but it was fraught with potential difficulties, and ill-conceived enough that if one element miscarried, the whole plan was likely to fail. On 27 February 1805, instructions were sent

Cadiz harbour. Villeneuve's Combined Fleet was blockaded here from early autumn 1805, at a time when the surrounding countryside was just recovering from an epidemic of yellow fever that had killed thousands of people and large numbers of livestock. The area experienced further hardship in struggling to meet the heavy demands of the fleet in the form of food, clothing, equipment and fresh water. (National Maritime Museum, Greenwich: PAH 2388)

to Missiessy, still in the West Indies, informing him to remain in place at least until the end of June, and then to make himself immediately ready to join other naval forces which would eventually reach Martinique. Besides those he expected from Europe, there were also half a dozen French vessels already waiting in the West Indies.

On the same day Admiral Gourdon, in command of the French fleet at Ferrol – four French and nine Spanish ships – was instructed to be ready to emerge from port and to combine with the squadron to appear from Brest under Vice-Admiral Honoré Ganteaume. On 2 March Ganteaume was told to embark approximately 3,000 troops, and to sail as soon as possible with his 21 ships of the line, six frigates, and two store-ships carrying supplies for Gourdon. He was ordered to proceed straight for Ferrol, chase away the blockading squadron under Sir Robert Calder, summon Gourdon by signal to emerge with his squadron, and together cross the Atlantic to Martinique where Missiessy and Villeneuve would be waiting. There they would reinforce the garrison with 1,000 troops.

Vice-Admiral Villeneuve, who commanded 11 ships of the line and six frigates at Toulon, was to elude Nelson's blockading squadron and sail through the Straits of Gibraltar to Cadiz, relieve the blockade there, bring out the Spanish ships trapped in the harbour, and sail for Martinique. There he was to remain for 40 days, awaiting the arrival of Ganteaume from Europe. If, after that time, Ganteaume had failed to appear, Villeneuve was to disembark his troops on French-held islands, attack British West Indian possessions, and then sail eastwards to take station off the Canary Islands, thereby posing a threat to British convoys bound for the East Indies or arriving from India, before returning to Cadiz. There remained the possibility that Ganteaume might rendezvous with him there, but if that admiral did not arrive within 20 days, Villeneuve was to return to Cadiz, where he would receive further orders.

Should Villeneuve fail to break out of the Mediterranean altogether, Ganteaume was to wait for 30 days when – though having only 25 ships of the line instead of 40 – he was nevertheless expected to reach Boulogne, fighting his way there if necessary. If he should find himself with even fewer ships, he was then to rendezvous off Ferrol, where all of the French and Spanish naval forces in European waters would concentrate before steering for the Channel.

If the plan worked as intended, this enormous combined fleet, assembled off Martinique, was to return immediately to Europe with the 40 ships of the line that Missiessy, Villeneuve, Gourdon and Ganteaume could muster between them. Off Ushant, Villeneuve, who would have numerical superiority, was to defeat any British squadron that he might encounter, and proceed north to Boulogne. His arrival was expected around mid-July. Once Villeneuve established command of the Channel, the invasion fleet could be launched and descend on the Kentish coast.

This scheme appeared simple enough in theory, but it was hopelessly ambitious, revealing Napoleon's ignorance of the limitations inherent in conducting naval operations. It was, in short, more the conception of a soldier than of a sailor. The Emperor took no account of the winds, which could potentially disrupt the time-table completely. Nor did he consider the consequences if even one of his squadrons encountered serious enemy resistance before they all had a chance to concentrate in overwhelming force. Campaigns at sea could not be planned like those on land, where the movement of troops and supplies could be calculated, if not with certainty, then with considerably more accuracy than that of ships. Thus the possibility of concentration and surprise was far easier to attain. The sea, always unpredictable, in an age when ships depended entirely on the wind, brought unforeseen problems and accidents, any one of which could throw Napoleon's entire strategy into disarray.

Napoleon inspecting ships at Cherbourg. If insufficient numbers plagued the French Navy, Admiral Ganteaume, commanding the squadron at Brest, informed his government of yet another problem, observing that the crews 'all lack the will, strength and courage to succeed'. The Emperor replied, acidly, 'Don't expect to get what we do not have [trained crews]; I cannot perform miracles.' (Alfred and Roland Umhey Collection)

Admiralty Board Room. In London the Lords of the Admiralty formulated plans for the ships and men of the Royal Navy whether on foreign station or in home waters. In planning strategy and in issuing orders both to fleets and individual ships, the Admiralty bore the awesome responsibility of managing the country's first line of defence. (Royal Naval Museum, Portsmouth)

Napoleon's plans were limited by his general's perspective of sea power, for in addition to his failure to take account of the fickleness of the winds, he operated on the assumption that the Royal Navy would do nothing to try to interfere with his plans until confronted by the combined – and numerically superior – Franco-Spanish fleet. He had seen how in 1798 Admiral Brueys had eluded Nelson between Toulon and Alexandria; he appeared to assume that, once again, his ships could reach their intended destination unmolested. His plan was considerably more complicated in 1805, however, and involved several squadrons, not only operating in different waters and under different conditions, but widely separated. If these various forces could unite they would indeed enjoy a numerical advantage over their opponents, but much depended on Napoleon's scheme succeeding as he intended.

The Brest fleet prepared to leave port on 27 March, while three days later Villeneuve emerged from Toulon into the Mediterranean.

BRITISH PLANS

An essential element of British strategy was the principle of blockade, which had been employed during the Seven Years War (1756–63). Confronting the enemy's main fleets at sea was not always necessary or even desirable, so that blockade played an important part in keeping enemy fleets at bay and required that Britain maintain a naval force at least as large as her two largest rivals, France and Spain, combined. Blockade not only prevented the enemy from interfering with British trade, it prevented it from receiving naval stores by sea or providing escorts for their own trade. By bottling up the various French fleets, Britain denied the enemy's merchant vessels access to France's colonies, from which she received a large quantity of her imports, and also prevented them from sending assistance to those colonies threatened or

Launch of HMS *Agamemnon*. It was as a young captain of the *Agamemnon* that Nelson first held command when war broke out with France in 1793. Of all the vessels aboard which he served, the *Agamemnon* proved his favourite. To his brother Nelson wrote: 'My ship is, without exception, the finest sixty-four in the Service...'. (Royal Naval Museum, Portsmouth)

attacked by British expeditionary forces. Thus, in the 1790s, British amphibious operations successfully occupied key French colonial possessions such as Tobago, Martinique, St Lucia and Guadeloupe, all the product of a strategy of blockade which permitted Britain to convoy troops across the Atlantic without fear of interference from French fleets. The strangulation of French trade also reduced merchant shipping and denied the enemy navy a source of trained seamen.

Blockade duty, by late 1804, was being conducted by Vice-Admiral Lord Nelson off Toulon with 13 ships of the line and 12 frigates; off Brest by Admiral Sir William Cornwallis with 33 ships of the line (though only about half a dozen of these were immediately deployed for blockade duty, while another six were on station off Ushant); and by other squadrons off Cherbourg, Lorient, Rochefort and Ferrol (this last being a Spanish port but containing five French ships). In the Downs, Lord Keith had 21 ships of the line and 29 frigates, though these were dispersed from the North Sea to Le Havre.

THE CAMPAIGN

The campaign of Trafalgar began when, with the collapse of the fragile Peace of Amiens in May 1803, Napoleon began to concentrate his army along the Channel coast in preparation for an invasion of England. In order to transport his army across the Channel, Napoleon needed naval superiority – even if temporary – in that narrow stretch of water, or embarkation of his forces would be impossible.

The task ahead was ambitious but not unrealistic. Dockyards across the Empire, from Holland in the north to Italy in the south, began feverishly building barges, while troops were withdrawn from various stations in the interior and along other coasts and shifted to the Boulogne area. Other forces were placed in reserve in northern France and Belgium.

The Admiralty took the danger seriously, as did the British public, whose fear grew to virtual panic over successive months. Militias across southern England drilled regularly and the government enlisted further recruits for defence. The burden of protecting the country, however, rested primarily on the Navy, and so long as Britain could control the Channel, the nation was safe. Yet no permanent solution to the problem could be found unless and until the French Navy was confronted and decisively defeated.

The first task of the Admiralty was to watch the French flotillas and block any attempt they might make at leaving port. Admiral Lord Keith, in command of a small squadron with headquarters in the Downs, supported by other vessels, operated out of Great Yarmouth and the Nore. A squadron of cruisers, under Captain Sir James Saumarez, stationed in the Channel Islands, served not only to form a link between Keith's squadron and the Western Squadron under Admiral Cornwallis, but also to prevent the French emerging from St Malo. The most important of the British forces was the Western Squadron, which performed three functions: to maintain a close blockade of Brest, to protect commerce, especially that approaching from the west, and to defend the Channel itself.

Nelson was given command of the Mediterranean Fleet, his primary duties to defend Gibraltar, Malta and the Kingdom of Naples, to monitor movement out of Toulon, engage the enemy if it should venture out and, above all, to prevent the Toulon fleet from combining forces with the French fleet at Brest. For over 18 months aboard HMS *Victory*, with Captain Thomas Hardy as his flag-captain, the vice-admiral never went ashore. During the course of his watch, he was informed in December 1804 that the Spanish and French had formed an alliance, thus increasing the strength of the French fleet by 32 ships of the line.

To oppose this new threat, the Royal Navy put Admiral Sir John Orde in command of a squadron with orders to operate between Cape Finisterre to the north and Gibraltar to the south, paying special attention to the port of Cadiz. Orde's appointment irked Nelson somewhat, for it divided his command, but he remained at his station, relatively content to watch Toulon, though his responsibility ought to have extended to Cape St Vincent.

Nelson's continued presence in the Mediterranean proved fortuitous, for, as we have seen, on 17 January 1805, Admiral Villeneuve, with 11 ships of the line and nine frigates eluded the blockade off Toulon. The French squadron in Rochefort had managed to manoeuvre out two weeks earlier; fears therefore grew that Napoleon's invasion plan was soon to be executed. Invasion was not, in fact, imminent, though neither the Admiralty nor Nelson knew this. Villeneuve was actually bound for the West Indies: the Emperor decided to postpone his invasion plans for the moment and focus on attacking British colonies in the Caribbean.

Nelson told two frigates to follow Villeneuve. They did so until they reached their rendezvous with Nelson's fleet off northern Sardinia, reporting from there that the Toulon squadron was standing south-south-west and thus providing more evidence to confirm Nelson's belief that the French were planning a descent somewhere on the Italian peninsula. Nelson therefore placed his fleet to intercept Villeneuve's progress east, only to be held up off southern Sardinia for several days by a gale, in the course of which he was joined by several other frigates bearing intelligence that suggested the French had taken one of two courses: either they had returned to Toulon or benefited from the wind, passing south around Italy and into the Aegean to menace Greece and then Egypt. In the belief that Napoleon wished to renew his operations in the Middle East, Nelson therefore headed for Alexandria.

In this theory Nelson was mistaken. As described earlier, Villeneuve's ships had returned to Toulon almost immediately, chiefly due to adverse weather. Meanwhile, Admiral Missiessy, who had escaped from Rochefort at about the same time as Villeneuve, had put to sea from Toulon, was steering a course for the West Indies with instructions to operate on his own and not wait for Villeneuve. The situation in the Mediterranean was left unaltered: the French fleet remained in port and intact, with Nelson continuing to maintain control of the Mediterranean.

THE CHASE TO THE WEST INDIES AND BACK

Napoleon now implemented his grand strategy: Villeneuve, Ganteaume and Missiessy were to rendezvous in the West Indies before returning to European waters, seizing control of the Channel and enabling the invasion flotilla to cross the Channel.

The Admiralty was aware of feverish preparations under way in the ports subject to British blockade. At this time Sir Charles Cotton replaced the ailing Admiral Cornwallis. His efforts to draw Ganteaume out of Brest failed, but on 19 April a British expeditionary force under Admiral Knight left Portsmouth for Malta, ultimately bound for Sicily, which was under threat of French attack. At about the same time, on 30

March, Villeneuve once again eluded the blockading squadron off Toulon and escaped into the Mediterranean.

Villeneuve did not know Nelson's exact location, but understood him to be off Barcelona, as a result of which intelligence he sailed east of the Balearic Islands. He was shadowed by two British frigates who believed the French admiral would encounter Nelson's fleet in the Gulf of Palmas (in southern Sardinia), a prediction that would almost certainly have been realized had not Villeneuve acquired information on Nelson's precise position from a neutral merchantman. Armed with this valuable knowledge, he changed course to manoeuvre through the Balearics, shedding the frigates following him and successfully evading Nelson's attempts to locate him.

On 7 April Villeneuve made contact with a Spanish squadron of six line of battle ships under Captain Alcedo. As Alcedo lacked orders to accompany Villeneuve to Cadiz, the French admiral, determined to lose no further time before Nelson discovered him, made for the Atlantic.

Admiral Orde was the first to hear of Villeneuve's escape and quickly withdrew towards the Western Squadron. His meagre force was no match for Villeneuve's, who had by this time anchored off Cadiz. Admiral Gravina immediately weighed anchor and the Combined Fleet proceeded into the Atlantic on the 9th, before British frigates could be organized to keep watch over its movement. This was superb news for the French, for whom the invasion of England now seemed a real possibility.

If spirits were high in Paris, they were certainly low in London as a result of unforeseen political developments. Lord Melville, the First Lord of the Admiralty, had been impeached and forced to resign from office on a charge of misuse of public funds, thus, for a short time, rendering the Admiralty without its senior administrator. Sir Charles Middleton was called out of retirement to fill the post. A former Comptroller of the Navy, Middleton (created Baron Barham), was nearly 80; a competent official, he took immediate charge, and was ultimately to emerge as the architect of the campaign.

Intelligence soon arrived in London that Villeneuve had managed to break out of the Mediterranean and had linked up with the Spanish. This gave cause for concern for Admiral Knight's expeditionary force. Villeneuve, his whereabouts unknown, could possibly locate and attack the convoy. Unaware that Knight had left England, Nelson remained in place. While off Majorca he heard of Villeneuve's escape from Toulon. Nelson knew nothing more until 18 April, while off Palermo, when he learned that the enemy fleet had passed through the Straits of Gibraltar about ten days earlier.

Nelson immediately steered a course for the Straits, but contrary winds meant that nearly a month passed before he could reach the Rock, where he then had the difficult choice between sailing north to reinforce the Channel Fleet or searching for Villeneuve elsewhere. When Knight's convoy anchored in the Tagus, in violation of Portuguese neutrality, Nelson was informed that Villeneuve had returned to Cadiz. This proved to be untrue, but it led Nelson to reinforce the convoy with the *Royal Sovereign*. Off Cape Trafalgar in early May he received correct intelligence that Villeneuve had collected some Spanish ships at Cadiz and was on a course for the West Indies. Nelson therefore began his pursuit across the Atlantic in search of the Franco-Spanish fleet. No

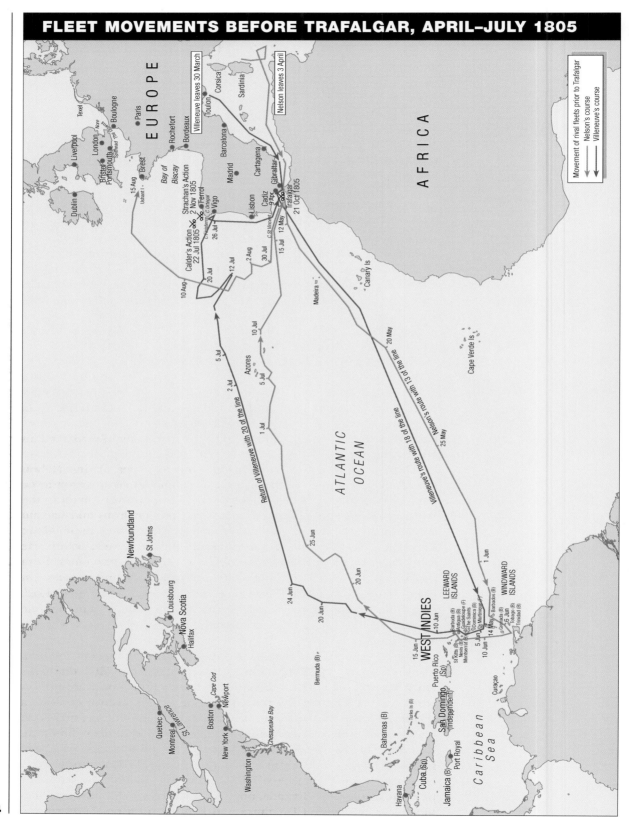

Movement of rival fleets prior to Trafalgar
Nelson's course
Villeneuve's course

EUROPE

AFRICA

ATLANTIC OCEAN

Caribbean Sea

WEST INDIES

Villeneuve leaves 30 March
Nelson leaves 3 April

Toulon
Corsica
Sardinia
Barcelona
Madrid
Cartagena
Gibraltar
Cadiz
Trafalgar 21 Oct 1805
Lisbon
Vigo
Ferrol
Bordeaux
Rochefort
Paris
London
Boulogne
Texel
Liverpool
Bristol
Portsmouth
Brest
Dublin

Strachan's Action 2 Nov 1805
Calder's Action 22 Jul 1805

Madeira
Canary Is
Cape Verde Is
Azores

Newfoundland
St Johns
Nova Scotia
Louisbourg
Halifax
Quebec
Montreal
Boston
Newport
New York
Washington
Bermuda (B)
Bahamas (B)
Turks Is (B)
Puerto Rico (Sp)
San Domingo (Independent)
Cuba (Sp)
Havana
Jamaica (B)
Port Royal
Curaçao

LEEWARD ISLANDS
WINDWARD ISLANDS
St Kitts (B)
Nevis (B)
Montserrat (B)
Barbuda (B)
Antigua (B)
Guadeloupe (F)
The Saints
Dominica (B)
Martinique (F)
Barbados (B)
St Lucia
Grenada (B)
Tobago (B)
Trinidad (B)

Return of Villeneuve with 20 of the line
Villeneuve's route with 18 of the line
Nelson's route with 13 of the line

20 May
25 May
1 Jun
5 Jun
6 Jun
10 Jun
14 May
10 Jun
15 Jun
20 Jun
24 Jun
25 Jun
20 Jun
1 Jul
2 Jul
5 Jul
10 Jul
12 Jul
15 Jul
20 Jul
26 Jul
30 Jul
2 Aug
10 Aug
15 Aug

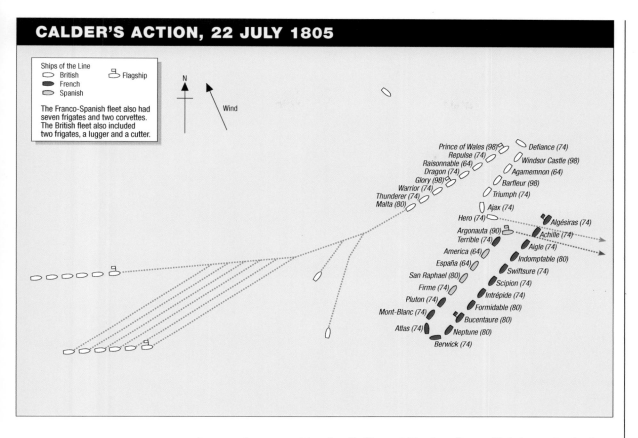

Ships of the Line
British
French
Spanish
Flagship

The Franco-Spanish fleet also had seven frigates and two corvettes. The British fleet also included two frigates, a lugger and a cutter.

N
Wind

Prince of Wales (98)
Repulse (74)
Raisonnable (64)
Dragon (74)
Glory (98)
Warrior (74)
Thunderer (74)
Malta (80)
Hero (74)
Argonauta (90)
Terrible (74)
America (64)
España (64)
San Raphael (80)
Firme (74)
Pluton (74)
Mont-Blanc (74)
Atlas (74)
Berwick (74)

Defiance (74)
Windsor Castle (98)
Agamemnon (64)
Barfleur (98)
Triumph (74)
Ajax (74)
Algésiras (74)
Achille (74)
Aigle (74)
Indomptable (80)
Swiftsure (74)
Scipion (74)
Intrépide (74)
Formidable (80)
Bucentaure (80)
Neptune (80)

longer threatened by the Cadiz and Toulon fleets, Knight embarked on 10 May, bound for Sicily via Malta.

Though their main fleet now plied the open sea leaving Nelson several weeks' sailing behind them, the French had good reason to be concerned. Admiral Missiessy had reached his rendezvous point in the West Indies, but had failed to find any other squadrons and had no choice but to return to Rochefort, where he arrived in mid-May. Villeneuve, meanwhile, had arrived at Martinique a week before. He captured Diamond Rock, a small British post a few miles from Martinique from which the garrison had been conducting raids against French merchant vessels. Nevertheless, the seizure of Diamond Rock took longer than expected, enabling Nelson to recoup part of the time he had thus far lost in his search for Villeneuve, who was four weeks ahead of his pursuer.

Villeneuve was in fact unaware that Nelson was looking for him. Instead, he believed that Nelson had remained in the Mediterranean. On 7 June, two days after the capture of Diamond Rock, the French admiral was joined by two ships under Rear-Admiral Magon. After a voyage of over 3,000 nautical miles, Nelson, meanwhile had arrived at Barbados on 4 June. Here he learned from General Robert Brereton, commanding on St Lucia, that a French fleet of 28 vessels had been sighted moving south in the direction of Trinidad. While not entirely convinced of the veracity of this information, Nelson nevertheless proceeded south. At Grenada, on 9 June, he was reliably informed that Villeneuve had passed Dominica and Antigua on a northerly course,

Nelson thronged by the public in the streets of Portsmouth. During his brief stay in Britain during the summer of 1805 the iconic admiral attracted large crowds of admirers and well-wishers wherever he went. (Royal Naval Museum, Portsmouth)

Nelson rowed out to the *Victory* at Portsmouth, 14 September 1805. This was the last he was to see of England. (Royal Naval Museum, Portsmouth)

capturing a convoy bearing sugar along the way. Nelson therefore altered course and returned north to learn that Villeneuve had anchored off Guadeloupe. With Nelson nearby, Villeneuve was unable to inflict much damage to British possessions and consequently set sail for Europe. Nelson duly set off in pursuit.

Having made no sightings of the enemy by the time he reached Collingwood's squadron off Cadiz on 18 July, Nelson disembarked at Gibraltar two days later, the first time he had set foot off the *Victory* in nearly two years. He and his men were greatly disappointed in having failed to bring the enemy to battle, conscious as they were that a massive enemy troop concentration remained encamped along the Channel coast.

Villeneuve was meanwhile approaching Cape Finisterre where, on 22 July, Admiral Sir Robert Calder's squadron, stationed off Ferrol, intercepted him and fought a confused and inconclusive engagement. Although Calder managed to capture two Spanish ships, he was reprimanded, for the action had interfered with Barham's plans by failing to divide the enemy fleet and thus had left the situation unaltered. As a result of this action Villeneuve put into Vigo on the 28th, then sailed further north and reached Ferrol on 1 August. Later still, he shifted the Combined Fleet again, to Cadiz on the south coast. Napoleon's plan to have Villeneuve's fleet combine with that at Brest and then make for the Channel had been spoilt.

Four weeks later, convinced that the French were bound for the Bay of Biscay, Nelson left Gibraltar and reached Spithead where, in spite of his failure to bring the enemy to battle, he was enthusiastically received. On 22 August he arrived at his home at Merton, in Surrey, where he remained with Emma Hamilton and their four-year-old daughter, Horatia. News arrived at the Admiralty on 2 September that Villeneuve had anchored with 30 ships off Ferrol. This was by no means favourable news, but it suggested that his then steering towards Cadiz rather than Brest had abated the immediate threat of invasion. Napoleon ended the prospect altogether for that year when at the end of August he broke up the camp around Boulogne and ordered the troops to march for the Danube to confront the Austrian and Russian armies moving west. The campaign of 1805 was now set to be fought both on land and at sea.

As the distance between the rival armies decreased, the rival fleets grew in size as they were reinforced by more squadrons. Nelson accepted overall command and on the evening of 13 September he left Merton for Portsmouth where he arrived early the following morning. Amid cheering throngs at the docks, he was rowed out to the *Victory* at St Helens, hoisted his flag and sailed down the Channel, accompanied by the frigate *Euryalus*. Nelson did not expect to return and had ordered to be made ready the coffin presented to him years before by one of his captains and fashioned out of the main mast of the French flagship at the battle of the Nile.

On the 17th he was joined by the *Thunderer* and *Ajax*. Six days later he reached Cape Finisterre, and on the evening of the 28th he reached the fleet under Collingwood and assumed command of the 22 ships of the line stationed off Cadiz, in which port the Combined Fleet continued to shelter.

NELSON'S TACTICAL PLAN

Nelson had devised a plan for engaging the enemy once it put to sea, which he issued as a secret memorandum to the various ships' commanders on 10 October. He would divide the fleet into three divisions. Two of these divisions would form up into two parallel columns, each attacking the enemy line at different points in such a way as to leave the van out of action. By sailing his ships headlong into the enemy, cutting their line at right angles about a third of the way down from the lead vessel and an equal distance from their rear, Nelson hoped to overwhelm the centre and rear of the enemy's fleet before its van could execute the time-consuming manoeuvre of going about and joining in the fighting. The third (reserve) division, in addition to any relatively undamaged vessels, would then confront the enemy's van if it should seek to join the battle.

By breaking the enemy line rather than pursuing a traditional 'line ahead' engagement with both fleets sailing parallel to one another,

Nelson explaining his plan of attack to his captains. In completely unorthodox fashion, he diverged from the traditional line ahead tactics in use since the 17th century by dividing his fleet into two columns and directing them to cut the enemy's line by driving straight into it. By thus isolating part of Villeneuve's fleet, Nelson sought to meet his numerically superior opponent on his own terms. (Royal Naval Museum, Portsmouth)

Nelson knew the battle would shift to individual ship-to-ship engagements – a general mêlée that Nelson had described in a conversation with a friend two years earlier as 'a pell-mell battle'. Nelson was confident of success. He believed he could justify such tactics on the basis of the superiority of his crews' morale, seamanship and gunnery. If, therefore, he could isolate a portion of the Franco-Spanish line, the enemy would be denied numerical superiority, British discipline and skill would prevail, and victory would be assured. Such tactics Nelson dubbed, in his characteristically arrogant fashion, the 'Nelson touch', a plan his captains not only 'generally approved, but clearly perceived and understood.' His subordinates, he continued in a letter to Lady Hamilton, received it '… like an electric shock. Some shed tears, all approved – it was new – it was singular – it was simple! and, from Admirals downwards, it was repeated – "It must succeed, if ever they will allow us to get at them!" '

When circumstances later changed, so, too, did Nelson's plan. As his fleet was not as large as he had expected – though it ultimately reached a strength of 27 ships of the line – and finding the enemy fleet numbering 33 line of battle ships, Nelson decided not to station the third division to windward. Instead, he would employ his entire force in two columns, one under his command and led by the *Victory* and the other under Collingwood in the *Royal Sovereign*, who was directed 'to make the attack upon the Enemy, and to follow up the blow until they are captured or destroyed'.

Nelson understood the immense risks that such tactics carried. By permitting the enemy to 'cross the T' – that is, exposing his leading ships to a deadly raking fire before they could bring their own broadsides to bear – and then plunging his vessels amidst the enemy with their rigging already damaged and their crews already reduced, the men would have to depend on their training and courage for survival and, hopefully, victory. Success would also depend on the certainty that every captain would continue in the wake of the next vessel ahead, each ship sailing a proper and swift course behind the ship leading the column.

Whether this plan may be regarded as intrepid or reckless is open to debate; for Nelson, however, anything short of daring was simply out of the question.

Nelson also understood that even the best-laid plans could go awry. He therefore offered simple, yet sensible, advice: '... in case Signals can neither be seen [n]or perfectly understood, no Captain can do very wrong if he places his Ship alongside that of an Enemy.' Here was the essence of Nelson's fighting philosophy: having himself devised the tactical plan which laid out the deployment of his ships, their companies were then to engage the opponent at close quarters and rely on the superior training and morale of the British seaman to prevail. Nelson's overall objective was also clear and simple, expressed in the letter he sent to Collingwood bearing his tactical memorandum: '... we have only one great object in view – that of annihilating our enemies, and getting a glorious peace for our Country.'

PRELUDE TO BATTLE

The Combined Franco-Spanish fleet had arrived in Cadiz on 21 August. Conditions aboard the ships were poor and relations between the two nationalities strained. There was insufficient food and supplies and both sides viewed the other with suspicion at best and contempt at worst, the Spanish maintaining that the loss of two of their ships in Calder's action the previous July had been the fault of the French. As time passed matters failed to improve.

At the end of September, Napoleon ordered the Combined Fleet to sail to Toulon via Naples. He was unaware of the strength of the British fleet off Cadiz and wrongly believed that his strategy of sending his squadrons across the Atlantic had successfully scattered most of the enemy ships in pursuit. Villeneuve, for his part, was displeased to find that he was to be replaced by Admiral Rosily (though Rosily would not appear on the scene before Trafalgar) and suspected, rightly, that Collingwood had been joined by Nelson.

On 2 October Villeneuve's fears were confirmed, and on the evening of the 7th he prepared orders for the fleet to sail. This was almost immediately countermanded, however, for strong winds, blowing in the wrong direction, would make steering a proper course impossible. When he was again prepared to weigh anchor, Villeneuve did not know the whereabouts of Nelson's fleet, for they had withdrawn out of sight, leaving only frigates to observe the ships in Cadiz. Villeneuve met strong opposition from his Spanish colleagues, who wished to remain *in situ*. Gravina maintained that the British would soon run low on supplies and, in any event, recently arrived reinforcements for the Spanish fleet needed time for further training. Arguments erupted, insults were exchanged, and Franco-Spanish co-operation threatened to collapse.

A decision was eventually reached by vote. The fleet would remain in harbour until bad weather gave it a reasonable chance of forcing the British to let it pass, or until such time as the enemy was forced to divide its forces to provide convoys for those merchant vessels entering the Mediterranean which might otherwise fall victim to the few Allied ships remaining in Cartegena and Toulon. Meanwhile, Nelson's fleet continued to grow in strength and by the time Villeneuve left Cadiz, the British force numbered 27 ships of the line.

When the Combined Fleet was prepared to sail, Villeneuve had a battle plan, though nothing of the order of Nelson's, which, remarkably, he anticipated. To his captains he warned:

The British fleet will not be formed in a line of battle parallel with the Combined Fleet, according to the usage of former days. Nelson, assuming him to be, as reported, really in command, will seek to break our line, envelop our rear, and overpower with groups of his ships as many of ours as he can isolate or cut off. All your efforts must be to assist one another, and, as far as possible, follow the movements of your admiral. You must be careful not to waste ammunition by long-range firing; wait and fight only at close quarters. At the same time you must, each captain, rely rather on your own courage and ardour for glory than on the admiral's signals. In the smoke and turmoil of battle an admiral can see very little himself; often he cannot make any signals at all.

On 18 October, Villeneuve ordered Admiral Magon, with seven vessels, including his own *Algésiras*, to put to sea with orders to capture the squadron under Blackwood, then on patrol off Cadiz, and to determine the strength of the larger force in the waters beyond. Yet when word was received that Admiral Louis had arrived off Gibraltar, Villeneuve countermanded his orders, for he now believed that the fleet sent to oppose him was still below full strength. He therefore gave the signal for the Combined Fleet to prepare to sail. Unfortunately for Villeneuve, when Magon's squadron left harbour he encountered becalmed conditions, rendering it impossible for him to return to port and obliging the entire Franco-Spanish fleet to emerge lest Magon's force be overwhelmed. As it happened, had Villeneuve managed to extricate his entire fleet quickly, he would have discovered the British scattered and unable to stop him from making a course of his choosing, winds of course permitting.

The Combined Fleet was clear of the harbour at Cadiz by 7am on the morning of the 20th, sailing south, watched by the frigate *Sirius* which passed the intelligence by signal in turn to *Euryalus*, *Phoebe*, *Mars* and finally to the *Victory*, then 50 miles west of Cadiz. Villeneuve's force numbered 33 ships of the line, a figure that Nelson could have matched had he not insisted on regularly sending ships to Gibraltar for provisions. Two were there on the 20th and four more were bound for the Mediterranean. Nelson, undaunted by the enemy's superior numbers, instructed the fleet to initiate a 'general chase' to the south-east and later gave the signal to prepare for battle.

The rival fleets, now fully aware of each other's presence, spent the 20th manoeuvring for the most advantageous position in which to fight the expected battle. Yet Nelson was in no hurry: he wanted Villeneuve to take his fleet as far from Cadiz as possible so that, once defeated – and Nelson had no doubts on this score – the enemy could not retreat and take refuge back in port. British frigates maintained contact with the enemy throughout the day and evening, transmitting constant signals to the flagship. Nelson kept his ships of the line out of sight over the horizon, proceeding on a parallel course 20 miles to the west.

Villeneuve found it difficult to keep his fleet in any semblance of order, a problem that had emerged from the very moment he had made the signal to his fleet to form in the order prescribed. His ships were supposed to be formed into three columns, but most of the men had no experience of sailing together as a fleet and could establish little more than a ragged line. The crews, many of whom were supplemented by soldiers prone to seasickness with no experience at sea, were themselves out of practice owing to seven weeks' enforced anchorage in Cadiz. Nor did the winds favour a direct course for the Straits of Gibraltar. Avoiding a confrontation appeared unlikely. Indeed, all prospect of escape vanished when at about 8.30pm Villeneuve received word that the British had been sighted.

On the morning of the 21st, Villeneuve was heading south-east, following the curve of the coastline towards the Straits of Gibraltar and away from the headland of Cape Trafalgar, south of Cadiz. Nelson now turned north-east and, keeping the wind behind him, narrowed the gap between himself and Villeneuve to ten miles. The two fleets now stood approximately 21 miles north by west from Cape Trafalgar. Villeneuve was dismayed to find the British fleet to windward of him and stronger than he had anticipated. With action imminent, Villeneuve sought to keep Cadiz under his lee in case he needed to seek refuge there. Yet his fleet remained in such disorder that when he hoisted the signal, 'Form Line of Battle', many vessels nearly collided while endeavouring to execute it. Franco-Spanish manoeuvres were poorly executed, with their ships crowded together, some to leeward, some to windward of their appointed stations, with many vessels sailing two or three abreast and part of the centre bulging to leeward. Gradually, however, the line formed into a rough crescent shape. The Spanish led the van as Villeneuve's fleet steered north.

Once he sighted Villeneuve's fleet, Nelson directed his ships, at 5.45am, to form two columns and make full sail. Each column was spearheaded by powerful vessels, with his own *Victory* leading the weather column, totalling 14 ships, and the lee line led by Collingwood's flagship, the *Royal Sovereign*, totalling 13 ships. Both divisions continued bearing down from the east, under orders, from 7am, to 'bear up and steer course East North East' and to 'Prepare for Battle'.

At 11am the two fleets were separated by only 3 miles, whereupon Nelson retired to his cabin to make a last entry in his diary, comprising a prayer and a codicil to his will in which he left Lady Hamilton as 'a legacy to my King and Country', requesting that in the event of his death the nation provide her with 'ample provision to maintain her rank in life … These are the only favours I ask of my King and Country at this moment when I am going to fight their Battle.' In his diary Nelson wrote: 'May the Great God, whom I worship, grant to my Country, and for the benefit of Europe in general, a great and glorious victory …' Lieutenant John Pasco, the *Victory*'s signal officer, found Nelson kneeling at his desk in the midst of writing. He told the vice-admiral that the ship had been cleared for action, whereupon Nelson visited the various decks with the ship's captain, Thomas Hardy, encouraging the men as he went.

The mood aboard the *Victory*, as in the British fleet generally, was ebullient, with the crew confident of success. Able Seaman John Brown recalled Nelson addressing the men: 'My noble lads, this will be a glorious day for England, whoever lives to see it.' He returned to the quarter deck amidst the cheers of his men. Many of the crews climbed the rigging to observe the enemy sail. Some cheered over the prospect of imminent victory, and on the decks of the *Bellerophon* the men chalked the words 'Victory or Death' on the barrels of their guns. Marine Second Lieutenant Ellis, watching the preparations for battle aboard the *Ajax*, was 'much struck by the preparations made by the blue-jackets [sailors]… The men were variously occupied – some were sharpening their cutlasses, others polishing their guns, as though an inspection were about to take place instead of a mortal combat …' Various captains exhorted their crews, including Charles Mansfield of the *Minotaur*, who told them: '… I trust this day will prove the most glorious our country ever saw. I shall say nothing to you of courage. Our country never produced a coward.' Captain Blackwood of the frigate *Euryalus* summed up the prevailing mood in the fleet: 'Almost all seemed as if inspired by the one common sentiment of conquer or die.'

Nelson at prayer before Trafalgar. On the morning of battle, he wrote in his journal: '… I commit my life to Him who made me, and may His blessing light upon my endeavours for serving my Country faithfully. To Him I resign myself and the just cause which is entrusted to me to defend.' (Royal Naval Museum, Portsmouth)

In sharp contrast to these sentiments, an atmosphere of doom hung over most of the crews of the Combined Fleet. Villeneuve, having abandoned any plan of attack or defence, and making little attempt to straighten his overlapping line, stood to meet an enemy he already anticipated beating him. Expecting Nelson to concentrate his attention on his rear division, Villeneuve had told his captains, 'In that case, a Captain can do no better than to look to his own courage and thirst for glory rather than to the signal of the commander-in-chief, who himself in the thick of the fight and shrouded in smoke, may perhaps be unable to make signals.'

As Nelson inspected the enemy fleet through his telescope he could see that it remained in a straggling line, slightly bowed towards the land, with his own two straight lines of ships making slow, yet inexorable, progress in the gentle breeze blowing from the west. Nearby, Dr William Beatty, the ship's surgeon, was quietly voicing his concerns over the vice-admiral's safety to Alexander Scott, the chaplain, for the admiral's frock coat had four chivalric decorations sewn to the front, making Nelson a conspicuous target. Beatty proposed to suggest that Nelson cover them. 'Take care, Doctor, what you are about', Scott warned him. 'I would not be the man to mention such a matter to him.'

It transpired that Beatty did not raise the subject, and in any event Nelson then ordered a signal hoisted at about 11.45am by which time, with the enemy now clearly in view, the opportunity for changing his uniform had passed. Nelson then addressed the signal officer: 'Mr. Pasco, I want to say to the fleet, "Nelson Confides That Every Man Will Do His Duty."' One of the officers tactfully suggested an alteration, changing 'Nelson' to 'England'. The vice-admiral agreed, adding, 'You must be quick, for I have one more to add, which is for close action.' Pasco, too, suggested a slight alteration to aid in communication. 'If your Lordship will permit me to substitute 'Expects' for 'Confides', the signal will be sooner completed, because the word 'Expects' is in the signal book, and 'Confides' must be spelt.' Nelson concurred

immediately. 'That will do, Pasco: make it directly.' Thus came into being the most celebrated signal in naval history, simple yet powerfully emotive: *England Expects That Every Man Will Do His Duty*.

The crews of the Combined Fleet could hear the cheers of their adversaries across the water. Some were eager for the fight, such as those aboard the crack ship *Redoutable* under Captain Jean-Jacques Lucas. 'Everywhere,' he later wrote, 'I found my brave fellows burning with impatience to begin'. But aboard the *San Juan Nepomuceno*, Commodore Don Cosmé Churruca anxiously watched the two enemy columns slowly advancing. Turning to his second-in-command, he prophetically described the fate that would befall the Franco-Spanish force and offered the antidote to impending disaster:

> *Our van will be cut away from the main body and our rear will be overwhelmed. Half the line will be compelled to remain inactive. The French admiral does not – will not – grasp it. He has only to act boldly, only to order the van ships to wear around once again and double back on the rear squadron. That will place the enemy between two fires.*

In disgust he declared 'Perdidos! Perdidos! Perdidos!' – 'We are lost, lost, lost!'

After prayers were offered by the ship's chaplain, Churruca, as if admitting that he must employ threats, addressed the crew: 'My sons, in the name of the God of Battles, I promise eternal happiness to all those who today fall doing their duty. On the other hand, if I see any man shirking, I will have him shot on the spot.'

THE BATTLE OF TRAFALGAR

Although they were making all sail, the progress of the British squadrons was laborious, and the first opening shots were not fired until noon, when, at ten past the hour, the *Fougueux*, 74, fired at Collingwood's lee division which was slightly ahead of Nelson's weather column. The French vessel's opening shots fell short, but with 60 ships of the line waiting to engage one another, a fierce struggle was certain to follow. With the British vessels flying their battle flags – white ensigns and Union Jacks – they gradually closed the distance with the Combined Fleet as Nelson's last signal – 'Engage the enemy more closely' – fluttered in the wind from *Victory*'s topgallant masthead. There it would remain until shot away.

THE LEE COLUMN

Collingwood led the lee column in his 100-gun *Royal Sovereign*, which, with the benefit of a newly coppered bottom, gave him a quarter of a mile lead over the next vessel astern and enabled her to avoid exposure to the enemy's fire for no longer than ten minutes before she reached the Franco-Spanish line. As he approached the gap between the *Fougueux* and the Spanish three-decker *Santa Ana*, the 112-gun flagship of Vice-Admiral Don Ignatius de Alava, Collingwood ordered his men on the upper decks to lie flat for safety and to hold their fire until ordered to do so. From the poop of the *Victory* Nelson, watching the scene through his telescope, declared with admiration, 'See how that noble fellow Collingwood takes his ship into action!'

The *Royal Sovereign* broke through the enemy line at approximately 12.20pm, firing her double-shotted broadsides into the stern of the *Santa Ana*, demolishing the ornate woodwork and putting several hundred men immediately out of action. She also raked the bows of the *Fougueux* as she broke the line, that ship's master-at-arms reporting later that the *Royal Sovereign* 'gave us a broadside from five and fifty guns and carronades, hurtling forth a stream of cannonballs, big and small, and musket shot. I thought the *Fougueux* was shattered to pieces – pulverized.' Still, her gun crews recovered from the initial shock and Captain Beaudouin's 74 answered with a broadside of her own. 'A well-maintained fire', the *Fougueux*'s master-at-arms continued, 'showed the Englishmen that we too had guns and could use them.'

A fierce duel of broadside against broadside then ensued between the *Santa Ana* and the *Royal Sovereign*: the engagement lasted for the next two hours at a range of about 400 yards. Aware that Collingwood would bear up on his leeward side once he broke the line, Alava shifted most of his gun crews to that side, delivering a broadside of such force that it actually made the *Royal Sovereign* heel out of the water. Over time, the superior training and gunnery of the British crew prevailed. According to William Robinson, Collingwood stood nonchalantly on his poop deck as musket balls and round shot hurtled past him, 'musing over the progress of the fight and munching an apple'. The *Royal Sovereign* took excessive punishment, being raked by the *Fougueux* and *San Leandro*, 64, and receiving broadsides from the *Indomptable*, 80, and *San Justo*, 74, unaided for nearly 15 minutes. So intense was the fire that round shot frequently collided in mid-air.

Relief for Collingwood came in the form of Captain William Hargood's 74, the *Belleisle*. She passed through the Allied line about 15 minutes after the *Royal Sovereign*, taking fire from eight or ten enemy vessels during the approach without replying with her own. Her upper deck crews were ordered to lie down between their guns, while the ship gradually sustained damage aloft. Three times her colours were shot away – and three times replaced by a sailor scampering up the rigging. Hargood was just one of Nelson's captains who refused to be intimidated, haughtily declining his first lieutenant's suggestion that he present a broadside before reaching the enemy. 'We are ordered to go through the line,' Hargood declared, 'and go through she shall, by God!' Passing through the gap between the *Santa Ana* and the *Indomptable*, the *Belleisle* opened her guns on the former's lee quarter, firing double-shotted grape from her upper decks before bearing away to rake the stern of the *Indomptable*.

Thereafter the *Belleisle* came to grips with the *Fougueux* in the course of which she was set upon by several other vessels, including the *San Juan Nepomuceno*, 74, which felled her fore topmast. The *Fougueux* then ran aboard *Belleisle* leaving the two locked ships together. In the fight that ensued *Belleisle* was mercilessly battered, losing her main topmast and mizzen mast. Then the French *Achille*, 74, standing off the *Belleisle*'s port quarter, joined the fight, but with her fallen mizzen mast hanging over the side, *Belleisle* could issue only an ineffective fire. Next to set upon her was the French *Neptune*, 84, which raked her; the *Aigle*, 74,

HMS *Belleisle* in a wrecked state. Captain Hargood's 74 broke through the Franco-Spanish line about 15 minutes after Collingwood's *Royal Sovereign*, but the long approach and the subsequent bitterly fought close action left her dead in the water, dreadfully pockmarked, and stripped of her masts, bowsprit, figurehead and anchors. (National Maritime Museum, Greenwich: Neg A5859)

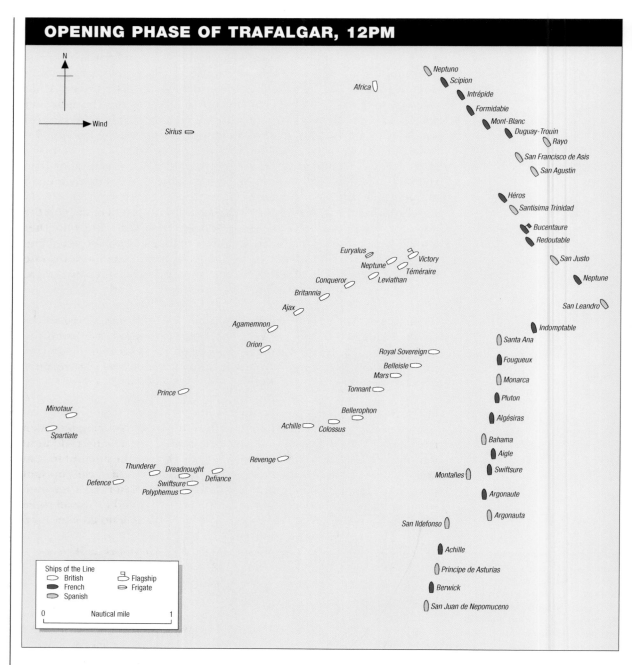

then appeared off her starboard bow. Together with broadsides delivered *en passant* by the *San Leandro*, *San Justo* and the formidable *Principe de Asturias*, 112, the *Belleisle* unquestionably took a greater mauling than any other ship in the British fleet.

Around 2pm the main mast of the *Belleisle* was shot away, her fallen sails obscuring the view of many of the portside guns. Thirty minutes later her fore mast toppled, and without her bowsprit, also shot away, she was reduced to a floating hulk. In spite of her predicament *Belleisle* continued to resist her assailants, her gun crews firing whenever a target appeared and whenever her batteries were clear of fallen sails, spars and rigging. All the while, to ensure that no one would mistake her for a prize, her colours remained nailed to the stump of the mizzen mast while a Union Jack flew defiantly from the end of an upright boarding pike.

The *Mars*, 74, the third ship in Collingwood's column, struggled to break through the enemy line. On his approach, Captain George Duff, believing that his ship would collide with the *Santa Ana*, brought her into the wind, leaving her stern exposed to raking fire. Despite support from the *Tonnant*, 80, the *Mars* received heavy fire from the *Monarca*, 74, and the 42-year-old Duff was decapitated by a round shot from the *Pluton*, 74, two seamen behind him being killed by the same shot. The Scotsman's body was left on the gangway until action ceased, covered in a Union Jack placed there by Duff's lieutenants.

The *Tonnant*, under Captain Charles Tyler, proceeded to take on the *Algésiras*, 74, and the *San Juan Nepomuceno*, the former entangling her bowsprit in the starboard main shrouds of Tyler's vessel and enabling the *Tonnant* to rake the deck of the *Algésiras*, a large number of whose crew assembled in an attempt to board the *Tonnant*. A lieutenant aboard the *Tonnant* described the scene:

> She had riflemen in her tops, who did great execution. Our poop was so cleared, and our gallant captain shot through the left thigh and carried below. During this time we were not idle. We gave it to her most gloriously with the starboard and main deckers, and turned the forecastle gun, loaded with grape, on the gentlemen who wished to give us a fraternal hug.

As Captain Magon of the *Algésiras* started to lead his men, a musket ball deprived him of his hat and wig, while another struck his right arm. Refusing to go below to see the surgeon, he renewed the attempt to lead his boarders when another bullet hit him in the shoulder. Still upright and urging on his men, Magon was then nearly cut in two by a round shot. His men were repelled and the *Algésiras* proceeded to lose all three of her masts over the side. A lieutenant on the *Tonnant* noted later how:

> The marines kept up a warm destructive fire on the boarders … We had the satisfaction of seeing her three lower masts go by the board, as they had been shot through below the deck, and carrying with them all their sharpshooters, to look sharper in the next world.

Quickly reversing roles, boarders from the *Tonnant* issued a cheer and carried their opponent, where they discovered the gallant Magon dead at the foot of the poop ladder and Captain Brouard severely wounded. Leaderless and unable to resist the torrent of screaming British sailors, the crew of the *Algésiras* struck her colours.

Aboard the battered *San Juan Nepomuceno*, meanwhile, Captain Churruca, though mortally wounded, refused to accept the inevitable, ordering the flag to be nailed to the mast and issuing explicit instructions not to give up the ship while he remained alive. His crew obeyed, yet so desperate was their plight that the moment their captain died they surrendered the ship.

Bellerophon, 74, under Captain John Cooke and next astern of the *Tonnant*, reached the enemy line a quarter of an hour later, engaging

Boarding. This scene demonstrates the ferocity of hand-to-hand fighting at sea, where the speed of events favoured the use of edged weapons over muskets and pistols, which could not be reloaded in the heat of combat at such close quarters. (Royal Naval Museum, Portsmouth)

the Spanish *Monarca* which, although she had struck her colours earlier, re-hoisted them when no British prize crew was sent to take possession of her. Cooke would have none of it, and sought to move under the stern of the *Monarca*, raking her as he went, before coming alongside to continue the fight. A crisis developed when at 12.35pm the *Bellerophon* fouled the *Aigle*, the former's fore yard locking with the French ship's main yard. Thus pinned, Cooke found himself under a deadly crossfire: from the *Monarca* on his port side, the *Aigle* on his starboard side, the *Bahama*, 74, on his larboard quarter and the *San Juan Nepomuceno* athwart his stern.

At about 1pm *Bellerophon*'s main and mizzen topmasts toppled over her starboard side, followed immediately by the main topsail and topgallant sail catching fire, ignited by the flash of the guns and the hand grenades continually hurled from *Aigle*'s tops. *Bellerophon* narrowly escaped destruction, as the first lieutenant described later:

> *One of these grenades in its explosion had blown off the scuttle of the gunner's storeroom, setting fire to the storeroom, and forcing open the door into the magazine passage. The same blast that blew open the storeroom door shut the door of the magazine; otherwise we must all in both ships inevitably have been blown up together.*

When *Bellerophon*'s ensign was shot away for the third time a seaman scrambled up the mizzen-rigging with a Union Jack and fixed it to the shrouds before descending to the deck. *Aigle*'s sharpshooters, poised in the tops and standing on the poop, could easily have shot him down, yet in apparent admiration of his intrepidity had withheld their fire. Cooke himself, however, was not spared, and was killed soon thereafter.

Sensing the moment was right, the men of the *Aigle* twice attempted to board, but as a midshipman of the *Bellerophon* recorded:

> *Our fire was so hot that we soon drove them from the lower deck, after which our people took the quoins out and elevated their guns, so as to tear her decks and sides to pieces … Her starboard side was entirely beaten in, so that she was an easy conquest for the* Defiance, *a fresh ship.*

The *Aigle* then fell astern of the *Bellerophon*, who raked the French 74 as she did.

The *Revenge*, 74, then came up in support of the crippled *Bellerophon*, raking the *Aigle*. Yet she soon faced the prospect of being herself boarded, as Robinson later described:

> *A Spanish three-decker ran her bowsprit over our poop, with a number of her crew on it, and, in her fore rigging, two or three hundred men were ready to follow; but they caught a Tartar, for their design was discovered, and our marines with their small arms, and the carronades on the poop, loaded with canister shot, swept them off so fast, some into the water, and some on the decks, that they were glad to sheer off.*

Over the next two hours the *Revenge* went on to engage several other ships, sometimes several at a time, leaving her hull riddled with shot holes between wind and water and rendering her virtually unmanageable. 'We were now unable to work the ship,' Robinson went on,

> *our yards, sails, and masts being disabled, and the braces completely shot away. In this condition we lay by the side of the enemy, firing away, and now and then we received a good raking from them, passing under our stern … Often during the battle we could not see for the smoke, whether we were firing at a foe or friend …'*

Despite her horrific injuries, *Bellerophon* was able to send a boarding party over to the *Monarca*, which had lowered her colours once again.

The *Colossus*, 74, under Captain James Morris, came through the line at 1pm, engaging enemy 74s on both sides: the French *Swiftsure* and the Spanish *Bahama*. *Colossus* eventually reduced the guns of the *Swiftsure* to virtual silence before pouring broadsides into the Spaniard, which, quickly succumbing, exchanged her own for British colours in token of surrender. While the *Bahama* was giving up the fight, the *Swiftsure* fell astern and manoeuvred under the stern of the *Colossus*. Morris nevertheless managed to wear his ship, so protecting her from the inevitably devastating effect of raking fire and at the same time bringing his own broadside to bear against his opponent. Soon enough the as yet unengaged *Orion*, 74, appeared, to add her weight against the *Swiftsure*.

ROYAL MARINES ON THE FORECASTLE OF THE *ROYAL SOVEREIGN* (pages 50–51)

Royal Marines issuing small-arms fire from the forecastle of the *Royal Sovereign* at the height of the action. Here (1) they deliver fire against opposing sailors and marines, gun crews, and sharpshooters positioned in the enemy's tops and rigging. Marines stationed closest to the bulwarks (2) could rely on a degree of cover from the tightly rolled canvas hammocks stuffed into the nettings running along the sides of the ship. Yet, exposed as they were on an open deck, they were subject to horrific injury from flying splinters, musket fire and grape shot, in addition to passing round shot, the wind of which alone could knock a man down – and sometimes kill him – if it passed close enough to his body. Those unlucky enough to find themselves in the direct path of a round shot (3) stood every chance of disfigurement and, more often than not, death. An officer (4) in his distinctive plumed hat stands by, with raised sword, shouting encouragement. In contrast to ordinary seamen (5), marines wore a uniform – and always full dress in battle. This consisted of a short-tailed, single-breasted, infantry-style scarlet jacket with stand-up royal blue collar and four-buttoned cuffs, white breeches, gaiters, round glazed hat with white brim, red and white plume, and pipe-clayed cross-belts (6). At Trafalgar most men still wore their hair in a queue, though this practice was officially abolished three years later. Royal Marines were armed with the standard sea service musket (7), a shorter version of the land pattern, and trained in infantry drill and tactics, not gunnery, though they did assist in manning the batteries when required. In action they were also stationed both above decks, in the tops as sharpshooters, and below decks, at the base of the ladders to prevent anyone from fleeing to the hold. In addition to issuing musket fire, marines always formed part of boarding parties. Over 100 marines served aboard the *Royal Sovereign* at Trafalgar. Marines and sailors had very little in common, though their different roles and characters generally complemented one another. One captain described their differences thus: 'No two races of men, I had well nigh said two animals, differ from one another more completely than the "Jollies" and the "Johnnies". The marines enlisted for life, or for long periods as in the regular army, and, when not employed afloat, are kept in barracks, in such constant training, under the direction of their officers, that they are never released for one moment of their lives from the influence of strict discipline and habitual obedience. The sailors, on the contrary, when their ship is paid off, are turned adrift, and so completely scattered abroad, that they generally lose ... all they have learned of good order during the previous three or four years. Even when both parties are placed on board ship, and the general discipline maintained in its fullest operation, the influence of regular order and exact subordination is at least twice as great over the marines as it can ever be over the sailors.'
(Christa Hook)

This proved too much for the French ship, which had lost her mizzen mast, and she surrendered. Though stripped of most of her rigging and sitting virtually dead in the water, the *Colossus* took possession of the *Bahama*, which had suffered horrendous losses – her captain dead and several hundred others killed or wounded – and the *Swiftsure*. The *Colossus* herself counted 40 killed and 160 wounded – the heaviest losses in the British fleet.

Thus, by 2pm – within just two hours of breaking through the Franco-Spanish line – Collingwood's division had practically defeated the enemy's rear squadron. It was a remarkable feat, but victory could not be assured without the success of Nelson's column.

THE WEATHER COLUMN

Forty minutes were to pass before the *Victory*, 100, and the ships astern came into action. Even at full sail her progress was slow as a result of light winds, and she received fire for 40 minutes without the ability to return any. Nelson had expected this as a natural consequence of his daring but risky plan. He was determined that the *Victory* should spearhead the weather division, so much so that when the *Téméraire*, 98, ranged up on the flagship's quarter, Nelson hailed her captain: 'I'll thank you, Captain Harvey, to keep in your proper station, which is astern of the *Victory*.'

Initially, Nelson could not make out the flagship of the Combined Fleet and had directed his officers and men to study the enemy line to identify her. Puffs of smoke and the flashes of guns appeared, splashing shot into the water ahead of the *Victory* and a few minutes later alongside her. Another shot plunged beyond her. At last, a shot tore through the *Victory*'s main topgallant sail, revealing the range to the enemy. As the

BELLEROPHON UNDER PRESSURE, 12.25PM TO 1PM

Captain John Cooke's 74-gun *Bellerophon* engages four enemy vessels simultaneously, principally the *Aigle*, a large proportion of whose crew consists of soldiers adept at small arms fire.

Note: Gridlines are shown at intervals of 91m/100 yds

▼ EVENTS

1 The *Bellerophon* crashes into the *Aigle's* larboard quarter, trapping her fore yard in *Aigle's* main yard.

2 The *Swiftsure* fires from her bows, but loses her commanding officer in the return fire. Cooke himself is killed by two musket balls to the chest and command devolves upon Cumby.

3 With the *Bellerophon* and *Aigle* locked in mortal combat at the closest possible quarters their respective gunners fight each other through the ports with muskets, cutlasses and rammers.

4 *Aigle's* sailors and soldiers assemble several times to attempt to board, but the gap proves too wide to render their design practicable.

5 Meanwhile, other enemy ships encircle the *Bellerophon*, the *Bahama* in particular inflicting considerable damage.

6 Caught in a deadly cross-fire, the beleaguered British ship ultimately loses her main and mizzen topmasts, while her deck and hull are riddled with shot-holes.

7 Against the odds, *Bellerophon* endures severe punishment, while the *Aigle*, with half her crew killed and wounded and her rate of fire drastically reduced, is obliged to pull herself clear of the action and limp away.

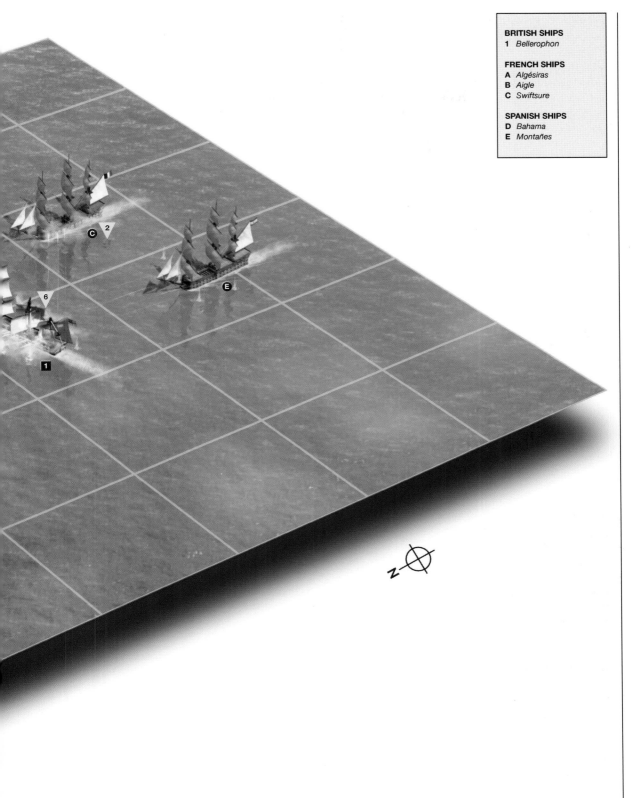

BRITISH SHIPS
1 *Bellerophon*

FRENCH SHIPS
A *Algésiras*
B *Aigle*
C *Swiftsure*

SPANISH SHIPS
D *Bahama*
E *Montañes*

Franco-Spanish line opened fire an array of ensigns and signal flags betrayed the *Bucentaure*, 80, which occupied a position about eleventh from the van. By 12.20pm the *Victory*'s sails were riddled with shot holes and the heavy, though erratic, fire was slowing her progress. When she came within 500 yards of the *Bucentaure*, the *Victory* lost her mizzen topmast and other round shot began to shred her studding sails. As the gap became narrower a round shot crashed into her wheel, obliging the ship to be steered by 40 men working the tiller in the gunroom, answering commands shouted down from the quarter deck.

Another shot struck and instantly killed Nelson's secretary, John Scott. His mangled remains were thrown overboard, while a double-headed shot knocked down a party of marines drawn up on the poop, killing eight of them and prompting Nelson to order the rest to lie prone. Another shot, penetrating the hammocks rolled in the nettings along the bulwarks, struck the quarter deck and sent a shower of splinters into the air, one of which tore off the buckle of Captain Hardy's shoe. Notwithstanding this punishment, *Victory* carried on, making straight for the centre of the enemy line. By now the signals flying from the *Bucentaure* clearly marked her out as the flagship, but Nelson did not at first steer for her. Instead, he made a feint by ranging along the enemy line, slowly moving toward the lead ships, making it appear as if he intended to pursue an orthodox line ahead engagement. A few minutes later, however, he ordered the *Victory* to turn and head through the smoke for the centre of the line, just as he had told his captains he would. 'How beautifully the admiral is carrying his design into effect!' Captain Edward Codrington of the *Orion*, 74, remarked as he observed the commander-in-chief now about to test the soundness of his own 'Nelson touch' in the rigours of combat.

On the *Bucentaure*'s starboard quarter stood the French *Neptune*, with Lucas's superb *Redoutable*, 74, on her port quarter. Captain Hardy could see that collision was certain and Nelson, agreeing, left him to decide on which he should run on board. At about 1pm the *Victory* plunged through the line under the stern of the *Bucentaure*, and ahead of the *Redoutable*. One carronade on the larboard side of the *Victory*'s forecastle, loaded with a 68-pound ball and a keg filled with 500 musket balls, was fired directly into a stern window of the flagship, causing clouds of dust and smoke to descend over *Victory*'s coughing gun crews. There were still 50 cannon left to fire as she passed and Hardy had ordered his guns double- and in some cases treble-shotted. The broadside that was fired into Villeneuve's flagship left her stern a smoking ruin, scores of men killed and maimed, and her interior strewn with wreckage. *Victory*'s approach was in fact so close that her main yard brushed against the *Bucentaure*'s rigging. Having wreaked havoc with her port broadside, the *Victory* then fired her starboard guns into the *Redoutable*, before putting her helm over to port and running on board her.

At about 1.10pm the two ships fouled each other[1], whereupon the men of the *Redoutable* lashed the ships together. A fierce action then developed between them. 'In less than a minute,' Lucas later recalled,

---

[1] The *Victory*'s starboard fore topmast studding-sail boom-iron hooked into the leech of the *Redoutable*'s fore topsail.

Victory cutting the line, viewed from the inside of the Allied line. Nelson's flagship was forced to endure 40 minutes of fire before this moment arrived. By then her wheel had been smashed and her mizzen topmast lost. Undaunted, she pushed between the *Bucentaure* and the next astern, the *Redoutable*, raking the stern of the *Bucentaure* at point-blank range and causing dreadful havoc. (National Maritime Museum, Greenwich: Neg 3167)

our decks swarmed with armed men, who rapidly spread to the poop, the nettings and the shrouds; it is not possible to say who was first. Then we opened a heavy fire of musketry. More than two hundred grenades were thrown on board the Victory, *with the utmost success; her decks were strewn with dead and wounded.*

Lucas, a courageous but diminutive man standing 4 feet 9 inches high, was not daunted by engaging his 74 against the 100-gun *Victory*, though he understood the dangers, having ordered the larboard lower deck gunports closed to prevent British sailors from boarding by that means. While the *Victory*'s port broadsides continued to fire into the *Bucentaure*, her principal attention was paid to the *Redoutable*, whose men threw grappling irons over the *Victory*'s rail, only to find that it rose too high above the bulwarks of their own ship. Though the difference in the height of the upper decks frustrated the boarders, it nevertheless proved an advantage for Lucas's marksmen perched in the fighting tops, for it shortened the range between the *Redoutable*'s tops and the *Victory*'s upper decks to a mere 50 feet. The marksmen poured down a devastating fire, supplementing the cannon and musketry from *Redoutable*'s main deck guns, the brass coehorns (small swivel guns) loaded with langridge (bits of scrap metal) mounted on the fore and main tops, and the men stationed aloft generously supplied with hand grenades, which they sometimes hurled down two at a time.

The *Victory* in return employed her starboard 68-pounder carronade to good effect against the men on *Redoutable*'s upper deck and fired into her hull at point-blank range with treble-shotted guns mounted on her lower gun deck. Above, on *Victory*'s upper decks, small arms fire and grenades

57

inflicted heavy losses, decimating the French crews, putting most of *Redoutable*'s guns out of action and forcing some of her men to seek shelter.

It was about this time, around 1.15pm, when Nelson, pacing the larboard rail on the quarter deck with Hardy, recognizable with his right sleeve pinned to his chest, his coat, though shabby, marked out with medals, was struck on the left shoulder by a musket shot and fell to the deck. A sergeant of marines and two seamen carried him below, while Nelson covered his face with a handkerchief in an unsuccessful attempt to conceal himself from the men as his bearers took him to the cockpit on the orlop deck. There he was received by Dr Beatty and Mr Burke, the purser. 'Ah, Mr Beatty,' said Nelson with resignation, 'you can do nothing for me. I have but a short time to live; my back is shot through.'

In the dim light Beatty had his patient undressed and examined him. He tried to probe for the bullet, but it had penetrated too deeply, and with no exit wound it appeared to have lodged in the admiral's spine. Nelson had no sensation in his lower body and with every breath he could feel a gush of blood, a sign of severe internal bleeding and probably a punctured lung. Severe pain in his backbone confirmed the location of the musket ball. He repeatedly implored the chaplain, 'Remember me to Lady Hamilton! Remember me to Horatia!' and called for drink and to be fanned. When Hardy arrived on the scene, Beatty explained in hushed tones that the wound was almost certainly fatal. The captain quickly made his way back to the quarter deck, where he assumed command. Collingwood would lead the fleet in the event of the commander-in-chief's death; but in the meantime, in accordance with Admiralty rules, the flag-captain acted on his behalf.

No sooner had Hardy emerged from below when a bugle blared aboard the *Redoutable*, followed by the cry, '*A l'abordage!*' The men were assembling to board. Most of the gun crews on the upper deck of the *Victory* had by now been killed or wounded, providing the French with the opportunity to carry the ship by direct assault. They gathered several times to make the attempt, but owing to the difference in the heights of the two vessels, found themselves unable to bridge the gap at upper deck level created by the tumblehome of the two ships; lower down, however, the vessels were actually in contact. Indeed, so close were they that *Victory*'s guns could not be pushed through her ports, and her sailors were obliged to thrust buckets of water through the shot holes made in the *Redoutable* to prevent fire from spreading to their own ship.

The intensity of the fighting was captured by Marine Lieutenant Rotely stationed on the middle deck of the *Victory*:

> *We were engaging on both sides; every gun was going off. A man should witness a battle in a three-decker from the middle deck, for it beggars all description: it bewilders the senses of sight and hearing. There was the fire from above, the fire from below, besides the fire from the deck I was upon, the guns recoiling with violence, reports louder than thunder, the decks heaving and the sides straining. I fancied myself in the infernal regions, where every man appeared a devil. Lips might move, but orders and hearing were out of the question; everything was done by signs.*

Each time the *Redoutable*'s boarders began to assemble, pistols and cutlasses in hand, they were held off with great gallantry by sailors and

Captain Jean-Jacques Lucas of the *Redoutable*. While this vessel remained blockaded in Cadiz, Lucas specially drilled his crew in small arms fire and boarding tactics which involved the use of grappling hooks and hand grenades. (Royal Naval Museum, Portsmouth)

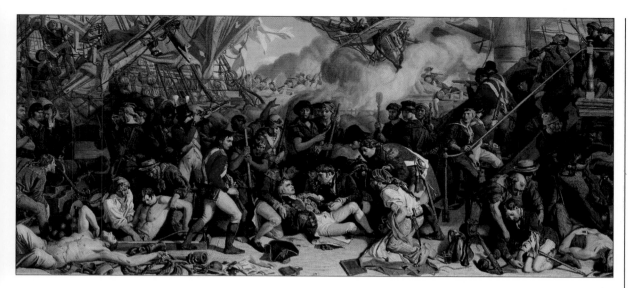

ABOVE **Nelson wounded on the quarter deck of the *Victory*. While tradition (and forensic science) has it that he was hit by a sharpshooter's musket ball fired from the mizzen top of the *Redoutable*, it is possible that Nelson was the victim of a stray shot. (Royal Naval Museum, Portsmouth)**

RIGHT **Nelson shot. No sooner had he received his wound, than he recognized its severity and declared his recovery impossible. (Royal Naval Museum, Portsmouth)**

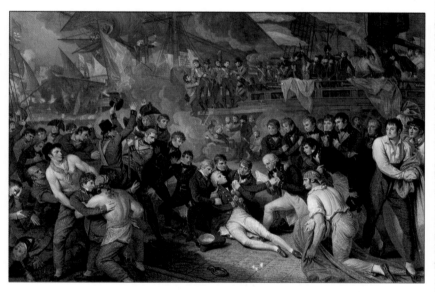

marines emerging from below at the critical moment, though they themselves lost heavily from small arms fire on *Victory*'s exposed decks in driving back the swarms of Lucas's eager men. Observing the problem and anxiously seeking a path for his boarding parties, Lucas ordered the supports of the main yard cut to create the necessary bridge. He was foiled yet again, however, when at that moment the two ships drifted against an unidentified vessel emerging from the gloom. It was another British three-decker – Captain Eliab Harvey's splendid 98-gun *Téméraire*.

The *Téméraire* was next astern of the *Victory* in the weather column and reached the enemy line only after receiving heavy fire in the same onslaught that much of the column had to endure during the approach. She followed the *Victory* under the stern of the *Bucentaure*, but in doing so was raked badly by the French 84-gun *Neptune* and left with few means of manoeuvring or making progress. *Téméraire* positioned herself with the *Redoutable* on her port beam, that vessel still lashed to the *Victory*, and

the *Neptune* on her starboard bow. While *Téméraire*'s starboard guns fired their deafening broadsides against the *Redoutable*, her larboard guns played against the gargantuan *Santísima Trinidad*, 140, and *Bucentaure*.

The *Téméraire* remained in this position until about 1.40pm when the *Redoutable* drifted on to her, the French vessel's bowsprit penetrating the main entry port of Harvey's ship, whose crew quickly seized the opportunity to lash down the bowsprit, trapping their opponent and pouring a regular fire into her bows. 'It is impossible to describe the carnage produced by the murderous broadside of this ship,' Lucas later wrote.

> *More than two hundred of our brave men were killed or wounded by it. Not being able to undertake anything on the side of the* Victory, *I now ordered the rest of the crew to man the batteries on the other side and fire at the* Téméraire *with what guns the collision when she came alongside had not dismounted.*

Sandwiched between two British three-deckers, the *Redoutable* carried on fighting, principally with small arms and hand grenades.

Téméraire then fired her starboard guns, which had hitherto remained silent, at the *Fougueux*. This vessel had earlier been exchanging fire with the *Royal Sovereign*, *Belleisle* and *Mars* of the lee column, but was now concentrating her attention on Harvey's beleaguered ship. The battered *Fougueux*, however, took great punishment from *Téméraire*'s broadsides, and after the French ship crashed into *Téméraire*'s starboard bow Harvey's men repeated their earlier procedure by securing the enemy vessel to their anchor. This left four ships locked side by side – the *Victory*, *Redoutable*, *Téméraire* and

Death of Nelson. Lying mortally wounded on the port side of the orlop deck, the hero of the hour is attended by the ship's surgeon, William Beatty. The stricken admiral lived for over two hours more in considerable pain, yet long enough for Captain Hardy to reassure him that a decisive victory had been achieved. (Royal Naval Museum, Portsmouth)

Fougueux, each furiously engaged with one another, while the *Victory* also continued to fire on the *Bucentaure* and *Santísima Trinidad* on her larboard side.

With the *Téméraire* abreast of the *Redoutable*, Rotely noted that special care had to be taken by the marines aboard the *Victory* lest they do harm to their consort:

> *It … became a great nicety in directing the fire of the musketry lest we should shoot our own men over the decks of the* Redoutable. *I therefore directed the fire of the marines to the main and fore tops of that devoted ship, and but few of their men escaped.*

But the *Fougueux*, still secured to the *Téméraire* on her starboard side, did not resist for long. The crew of the *Téméraire* boarded and forced her to capitulate after ten minutes' resistance.

By this time, about 2pm, the *Victory* had managed to boom herself off from *Redoutable* and move slowly northward, leaving her, the *Téméraire* and the *Fougueux*, to drift to the south. The *Redoutable*, her stern on fire, lost her main and mizzen masts, the latter falling across the deck of the *Téméraire*, whose men used it to board, and at about 2.20pm they took possession of the ship. 'I no longer hesitated about surrendering', Lucas wrote later. 'The leaks were serious enough to sink the ship, so the enemy would not have her long.' Of her original strength of 643, 300 men aboard the *Redoutable* were dead and over 200 lay wounded.

The British *Neptune* passed through the line ahead of the *Victory* and under the stern of the *Santísima Trinidad*, whose 140 guns mounted on four decks made her easily the largest ship at Trafalgar – or indeed anywhere. Undaunted, Captain Thomas Fremantle luffed up his 98-gun three-decker alongside the Spanish behemoth and fought her. A few minutes before 2pm, amidst a deafening crash, her masts collapsed, leaving her, in the words of an officer of the *Conqueror*, 74, 'an unmanageable hulk … and the falling of this mass of spars, sails, and rigging, plunging into the water at the muzzles of our guns, was one of the most magnificent sights I ever beheld.' During her approach the *Neptune* had passed under *Bucentaure*'s stern, followed by the *Leviathan*, 74, and then the *Conqueror*, all of whom fired successively into the rear of the Allied flagship.

At about this time Villeneuve, anxious that he must have the support of those ships of his fleet that were not yet in action, sought by signal to order them to enter the fray and engage the enemy as swiftly as possible. He was mainly concerned to communicate with Admiral Dumanoir Le Pelley's van division, which was still standing on. He frantically signalled for Dumanoir to reverse course, but the latter did nothing for more than an hour – a fatal error that he attributed to his inability to make out the signal in the smoke of battle. The fact that Dumanoir could see that the entire British fleet

The mighty *Santísima Trinidad*, the pride of the Spanish Navy. With 140 guns mounted on four decks, she easily out-classed every other ship afloat. Weaponry alone, however, failed to compensate for the generally mediocre quality of her crew – a shortcoming that plagued most of her consorts in the Combined Fleet. (Alfred and Roland Umhey Collection)

FRENCH SHARPSHOOTERS IN THE MIZZEN TOP OF THE REDOUTABLE (62–63)

French sharpshooters perched in the mizzen top of the *Redoutable* direct a rain of fire down on the quarter deck of the *Victory*. While blockaded at Cadiz, Captain Lucas had specially trained his crew in small-arms drill and grenade-throwing. His opportunity to exploit this training came at Trafalgar when the *Victory* pushed between the *Bucentaure* and her next astern – the *Redoutable* – and managed to foul her studding-sail iron on the foretopsail of Lucas's vessel. The higher deck of the *Victory* gave the men of the *Redoutable* an advantage, shortening the range from their mizzen platform to the *Victory*'s upper decks to only fifty feet. Even so, the two ships rolled with the swells and shook at the recoil of the broadsides. Visibility for the sharp-shooters was partly obscured by criss-crossing rigging, splintered yardarms, tattered sails and drifting clouds of smoke. Nevertheless, below, near the larboard rail, with one sleeve pinned to the front of his frock coat and wearing the distinctively shaped admiral's hat, stood a diminutive yet most conspicuous target: Lord Nelson. The mizzen mast was considerably smaller than the other two (the main and fore masts), and was situated on the quarter deck, towards the rear of the ship. Each mast had a top – a broad, flat, D-shaped platform – situated about a third of the way up the mast from the upper deck, and from which men could work in the rigging or, in action, issue musket fire. A marine (1) rams a musket ball down the muzzle of his weapon, while in front of him a sailor (2) discharges his musket, creating the thick white smoke produced by the ignition of the crude black powder in use at the time – a composite of sulphur,

saltpetre (potassium nitrate) and fine charcoal. Two other seamen (3) take aim, too occupied to attend to their wounded comrade (4), struck down by opposing musket fire. Another sailor (5) climbs the ratlines – a sort of light rope ladder tied along the shrouds – though access to the top could also be made through the 'lubber's hole' in the centre of the platform. The shrouds constituted part of the standing rigging, which supported the masts and ran from the ship's sides. The identity of the man who shot Nelson will probably never be known, but according to the *Victory*'s surgeon, William Beatty, whoever he was he did not live to boast of his feat. 'It is by no means certain, though highly probable,' Beatty wrote in his account of the admiral's death, 'that Lord Nelson was particularly aimed at by the Enemy. There were only two Frenchmen left alive in the mizzen-top of the *Redoutable* at the time of his Lordship's being wounded, and by the hands of one of these he fell. These men continued firing at Captains Hardy and Adair, Lieutenant Rotely of the Marines, and some of the Midshipmen on the *Victory*'s poop, for some time afterwards. At length one of them was killed by a musket-ball, and on the other's then attempting to make his escape from the top down the rigging, Mr Polland (Midshipman) fired his musket at him, and shot him in the back, when he fell dead from the shrouds, on the *Redoutable*'s poop.' According to other contemporary sources, when Midshipmen Collingwood and Pollard went aboard the *Redoutable* after it had become a prize, they found in the mizzen top the man whom they had apparently shot simultaneously, with a musket-ball wound in his head and another in his chest. (Christa Hook)

was engaging a smaller number of Franco-Spanish ships in the centre and rear did not appear to influence him. He had his orders, and may have presumed that Villeneuve intended to keep his van in reserve. Dumanoir's last instructions were to sail a straight course. Fortunately for Nelson, that is precisely what he did.

For Villeneuve, therefore, it was too late. Standing virtually alone on the quarter deck of the *Bucentaure*, his ship sat crippled and mastless, his officers shot down around him, the cockpit heaving with 450 wounded, and the surgeon and his mates overwhelmed with work. The ship's boats were all smashed to pieces, making it impossible for him to be rowed to another ship. When the beleaguered *Santísima Trinidad* failed to reply to his signal to send a boat, Villeneuve recognized the futility of fighting on. 'I had to yield to my destiny', he reported later. Ordering the colours lowered at about 2pm, he presented his sword to Captain of Marines James Atcherley of the *Conqueror*, who with five others was sent on board to take custody of the admiral (ultimately taken to the *Mars*) who had miraculously remained unscathed amidst the destruction. Atcherley described the gun decks' appearance thus:

> *The dead, thrown back as they fell, lay along the middle of the decks in heaps, and the shot passing through these, had frightfully mangled the bodies … More than four hundred had been killed and wounded, of whom an extraordinary proportion had lost their heads. A raking shot, which entered the lower deck, had glanced along the beams and through the thickest of the people, and a French officer declared that this shot alone had killed or disabled nearly forty men.*

By this time the battle was reaching its climax, roughly divided into two separate actions in the centre and rear of the now shattered Franco-Spanish line. While a decisive British victory was the likely outcome of the ferocious fighting which had only commenced two hours before, securing that victory now depended on the ability of the British to stave off any attack from the Allied ships thus far unengaged – the ten ships of the van under Dumanoir, still proceeding north – and to capture as many of the remaining ships of the centre and rear as possible.

CLOSING PHASE

By 3.30pm, even as more British ships were coming into action, the fight in the centre and rear of the Allied line was virtually over, with the **65**

SITUATION OF LEADING VESSELS OF NELSON'S COLUMN, 1.15PM TO 1.45PM

Note: Gridlines are shown at intervals of 91m/100yds

▼ EVENTS

1 **Having pierced the enemy line and raked the stern of the *Bucentaure*, the *Victory* engages the *Redoutable* at close range and forces her slightly off to leeward. The two ships are lashed together by the French who intend to board. Nelson falls mortally wounded at approximately 1.15pm.**

2 ***Téméraire*, second in the line, moves round the stern and comes alongside of the *Redoutable*, whom she engages at approximately 1.25pm.**

3 **The third vessel in Nelson's column, the *Neptune*, follows through the gap, passing between the *Victory* and *Bucentaure*, firing at the latter's stern as she proceeds.**

4 **Villeneuve's flagship, the *Bucentaure*, receives devastating broadsides to her stern from both the *Victory* and *Neptune* as those vessels pass through the Franco-Spanish line. Villeneuve repeats his earlier order for Dumanoir's van squadron to join the action in order to save the fleet from being overwhelmed.**

5 **The massive *Santísima Trinidad* receives a devastating raking broadside to her stern from the *Neptune*, which then luffs up to her starboard quarter to exchange fire at close range.**

6 ***Leviathan*, fourth in Nelson's line, follows in the wake of the British *Neptune*, firing a raking broadside into the stern of the** *Bucentaure* before coming round to larboard to deliver another broadside. She then seeks out the French ship *Neptune*, which quickly flees to leeward.

7 ***Conqueror*, fifth in Nelson's line, steers under the stern of the *Bucentaure*, issuing crushing broadsides into her stern before luffing round to larboard and bringing-to on her opponent's starboard quarter, forcing her to surrender. *Conqueror* then proceeds to engage the formidable *Santísima Trinidad* on her windward side.**

8 ***Britannia*, next astern of the *Conqueror*, unleashes broadsides into the *Bucentaure* only minutes before the French flagship strikes her colours. *Britannia* then joins the attack on the *Santísima Trinidad*.**

9 ***Africa* approaches the *Santísima Trinidad* and engages her on the weather bow.**

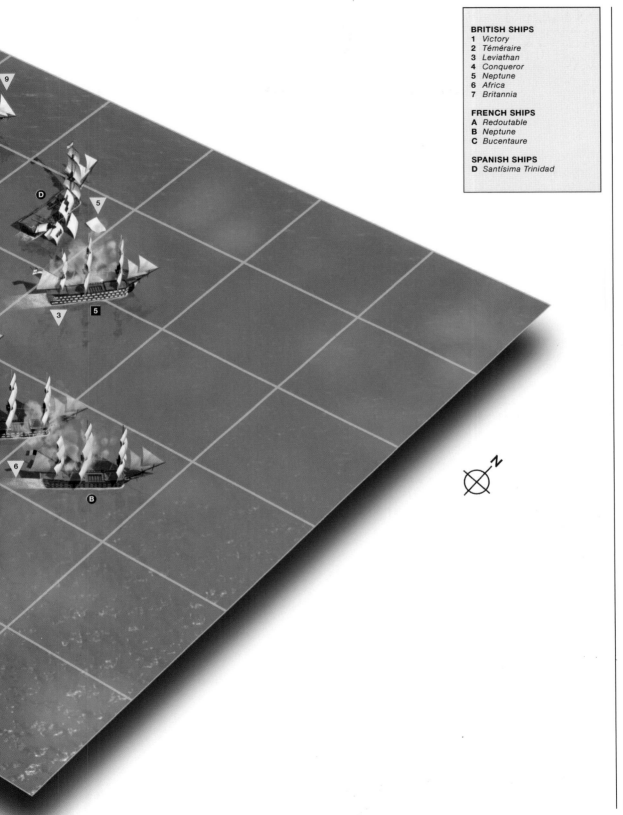

BRITISH SHIPS
1 *Victory*
2 *Téméraire*
3 *Leviathan*
4 *Conqueror*
5 *Neptune*
6 *Africa*
7 *Britannia*

FRENCH SHIPS
A *Redoutable*
B *Neptune*
C *Bucentaure*

SPANISH SHIPS
D *Santísima Trinidad*

British clearly having the upper hand, though several of their ships had been severely mauled. The *Belleisle*, which had at various times received sustained and intensive fire from at least nine enemy ships, was dead in the water. She was fortunate that the *Swiftsure*, 74, and *Polyphemus*, 64, came to her relief after almost four hours' continuous resistance. Exhausted, the crew of the *Belleisle* could at last cease firing and turn their attention to clearing the wreckage lying across the decks and hanging over the sides of the ship. She had not a stick standing, nor a bowsprit or figurehead. Yet even she could take a prize, the Spanish *Argonauta*, 80, which had hoisted a British flag to indicate a desire to strike. Amazingly, the *Belleisle* found a seaworthy boat and took aboard the Spaniard's commander, who joined Hargood and his officers for tea in the captain's cabin.

In the course of the fighting, the gigantic *Santísima Trinidad* had been set upon by several British ships. After her colours were shot away and her guns silenced, Captain Henry Digby of the *Africa*, 64, sent over a boat to accept her surrender. When the party approached they found Rear-Admiral Don Hidalgo Cisneros wounded, together with his two senior officers, but another officer politely informed the British that the ship intended to fight on. With a courtesy characteristic of the times, the British officer was escorted back to his boat and the Spanish vessel's gunners withheld their fire until the enemy had returned aboard the *Africa*. Fighting then resumed, but in the end the Spanish resigned themselves to their fate, a sailor displaying a Union Jack on the lee gangway in token of surrender.

By this point, according to Perez Galdos, a member of her crew, the former pride of the Spanish Navy looked like a charnel house.

She could not move. The English shot had torn our sails to tatters. It was as if huge invisible talons had been dragging at them. Fragments of spars, splinters of wood, thick hempen cables cut up as corn is cut by the

Trafalgar. Superior British tactics, gunnery, seamanship, morale and the inspiration provided by history's greatest admiral more than compensated for the Allies' numerical superiority in ships, men, and guns. (Royal Naval Museum, Portsmouth)

sickle, fallen blocks, shreds of canvas, bits of iron, and hundreds of other things that had been wrenched away by the enemy's fire were piled along the deck. Blood ran in streams about the deck, and in spite of the sand the rolling of the ship carried it hither and thither until it made strange patterns on the planks. The ship creaked and groaned as she rolled, and through a thousand holes and crevices in her hull the sea spurted in and began to flood the hold.

When Midshipman Babcock of the *Neptune* went aboard as part of the prize crew he discovered 'between three and four hundred killed and wounded; her beams were covered with Blood, Brains and pieces of Flesh and the after part of her Decks with wounded, some without legs and some without an Arm.'

Rear-Admiral Dumanoir, meanwhile, still unengaged, now responded to Villeneuve's signals, either because he had finally recognized the commander-in-chief's signal flags – though these had been flown throughout the action by other vessels – or because he realized that he would face court martial and probable death if he failed to obey the order. When he finally chose to act, it was nearly two hours after the battle had begun, and he was hampered by lack of wind, which meant boats were needed to tow his ships, including his own *Formidable*, 80, around.

Dumanoir's plan to rejoin the fleet dissolved in farce. Of the ten ships he had with him – the original seven of his division, plus the *Intrépide*, *Héros* and the *San Agustín* – only five (*Formidable*, *Duguay-Trouin*, *Scipion* and *Mont-Blanc*, followed at a distance by *Neptuno*) were able to come about and attempt to join the fighting directly under his control. These sailed down the weather side of the line to assist the centre, while the remaining five vessels sailed to leeward in an effort to relieve Admiral Gravina's rear division. In the process two 74s, the *Intrépide* and *Mont-Blanc*, collided, shearing off the former's jib boom and splitting the latter's foresail. Two Spanish ships drifted to the east, leaving Dumanoir, with nothing more than a gentle breeze, to struggle for more than an hour to move his five ships to the scene of action.

The *Ajax*, 74, and *Agamemnon*, 64, fired at the van, but they could not of themselves stop it. However, Collingwood, now aware of Nelson's death, had assumed command of the fleet and signalled the weather division to form a line to intercept Dumanoir's ships. Lack of visibility as a result of smoke, or being occupied in the battle, meant that only seven ships (*Leviathan*, *Conqueror*, *Britannia*, *Africa*, *Neptune*, *Ajax* and *Agamemnon*) responded to the call, but these formed a crude line, so convincing Dumanoir that he could not support the Allied rear without fighting his way through – with no certainty that even this was possible.

Two British 74s, the *Minotaur* and the *Spartiate*, both of the weather column and as yet unengaged, perceived the impending threat, especially to those of their severely damaged consorts who were unable to defend themselves against fresh assailants. Chief amongst these were the *Victory* and *Téméraire*, little more than hulks by this time. *Minotaur* and *Spartiate* daringly crossed the path of Dumanoir's five vessels and raked the bows of the vice-admiral's flagship at point blank range. The two British ships then blocked their opponents' progress, protecting the shattered *Victory*, and exchanging fire. They also managed to isolate the Spanish 80-gun

FINAL STAGE BEGINS, 2.45PM TO 3.15PM

11 French and Spanish ships have surrendered.

Note: Gridlines are shown at intervals of 183m/200yds

FRENCH SHIPS
A *Formidable*
B *Duguay-Trouin*
C *Scipion*
D *Mont-Blanc*
E *Intrépide*
F *Héros*
G *Bucentaure*
H *Indomptable*
I *Fougueux*
J *Redoutable*
K *Argonaute*
L *Swiftsure*
M *Neptune*
N *Pluton*
O *Algésiras*
P *Aigle*
Q *Berwick*
R *Achille*

SPANISH SHIPS
S *Neptuno*
T *Rayo*
U *San Francisco de Asís*
V *San Agustín*
W *Santísima Trinidad*
X *Montañes*
Y *Santa Ana*
Z *Bahama*
AA *San Leandro*
BB *San Justo*
CC *Principe de Asturias*
DD *San Ildefonso*
EE *San Juan Nepomuceno*
FF *Monarca*
GG *Argonauta*

BRITISH FLEET

VICE-ADMIRAL VISCOUNT NELSON

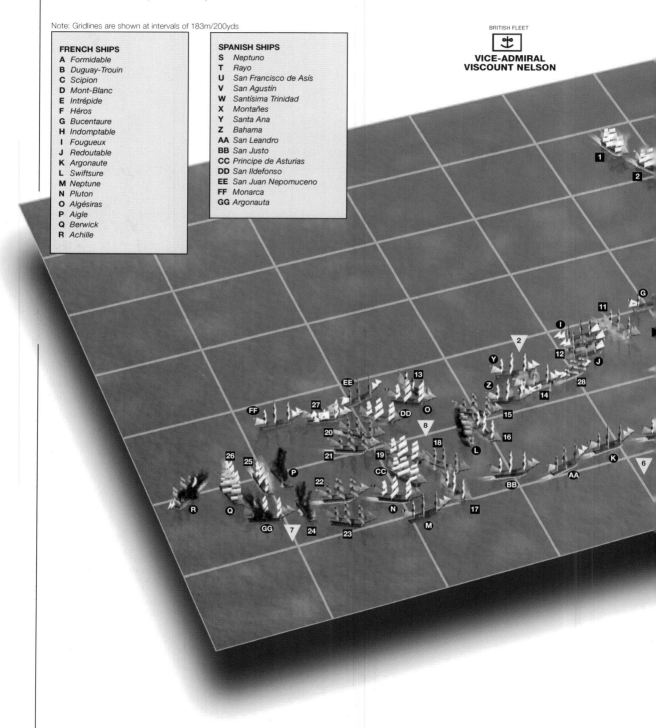

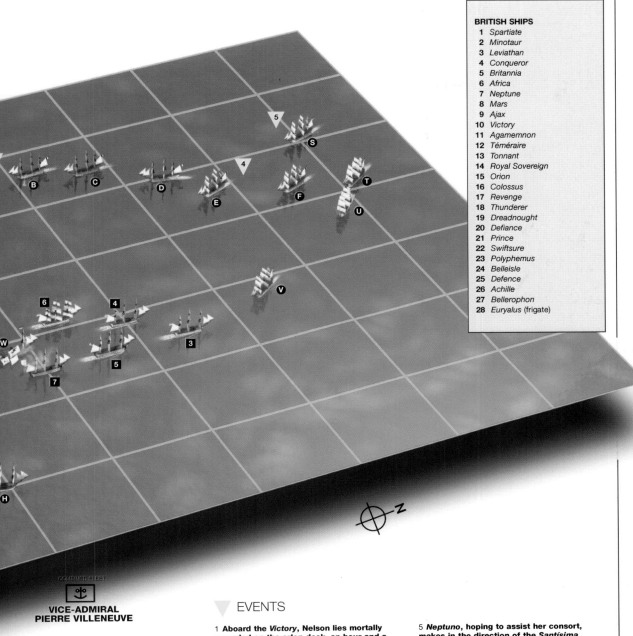

71

BRITISH SHIPS
1 Spartiate
2 Minotaur
3 Leviathan
4 Conqueror
5 Britannia
6 Africa
7 Neptune
8 Mars
9 Ajax
10 Victory
11 Agamemnon
12 Téméraire
13 Tonnant
14 Royal Sovereign
15 Orion
16 Colossus
17 Revenge
18 Thunderer
19 Dreadnought
20 Defiance
21 Prince
22 Swiftsure
23 Polyphemus
24 Belleisle
25 Defence
26 Achille
27 Bellerophon
28 Euryalus (frigate)

COMBINED FLEET

**VICE-ADMIRAL
PIERRE VILLENEUVE**

▼ EVENTS

1 Aboard the *Victory*, Nelson lies mortally wounded on the orlop deck, an hour and a half after being hit.

2 Several British ships drifting out of control, very badly damaged. The *Royal Sovereign*, *Tonnant*, *Mars*, and *Bellerophon* are unable to set sail.

3 The van of the Combined Fleet, under Dumanoir Le Pelley, has tacked but is not yet in action and is too late to assist the Franco-Spanish centre and rear. Instead of steering straight for the main scene of action, Dumanoir sails half a mile to windward, followed by only three of his ships, all French.

4 *Intrépide*, under Captain Infernet, sets a course directly for the *Bucentaure*, Villeneuve's flagship, which he hopes to assist.

5 *Neptuno*, hoping to assist her consort, makes in the direction of the *Santísima Trinidad*.

6 *Indomptable* and some Spanish vessels try to escape by running to leeward.

7 The *Belleisle*, completely dismasted, continues to resist all opponents.

8 *Dreadnought*, having forced the *San Juan Nepomuceno* to lower her colours, proceeds to engage Gravina's flagship, the *Principe de Asturias*.

The French 74, *Achille*, ablaze. A broadside brought down her main mast, already in flames, spreading fire across her decks and then below. At 5.45pm she exploded, by which time only one-fifth of her 500-man crew had been saved by HMS *Prince*. (National Maritime Museum, Greenwich: PAD 4046)

Neptuno, which was both a fair distance astern and to leeward of the others. After resisting for an hour the Spaniard capitulated.

Meanwhile, in the cockpit of the *Victory*, at about 4pm Hardy reported to Nelson that his fleet had won a great victory, having captured 14 or 15 vessels. 'That is well,' the admiral replied, 'but I bargained for 20.' A short time later he whispered to Scott: 'Thank God I have done my duty.' He then requested a kiss from Hardy, who knelt down and kissed the admiral's cheek and forehead – not, under the circumstances, an unusual gesture of fraternal affection in the pre-Victorian age. 'God bless you, Hardy!' Nelson whispered and, shortly thereafter, at 4.30pm, he died. In the log of the *Victory*, the midshipman of the watch pencilled in the bitter-sweet results of the battle: 'Partial firing continued until 4.30, when a victory having been reported to the Right Hon. Lord Viscount Nelson, K. B., and Commander-in-Chief, he died of his wound.'

Aboard the Spanish flagship, the *Principe de Asturias*, Gravina, his left arm shattered, his main mast and mizzen mast on the point of collapsing and aware that the *Bucentaure* and *Santísima Trinidad* had given up, realized that escape was the only option if he wished to avoid the same fate. The frigate *Thémis*, 40, took him in tow, and he signalled all the other ships capable of making sail to follow him in a dash for Cadiz. In the event, 11 ships of the line managed to follow.

Sighting Gravina's improvised squadron fleeing the scene of action and steering away for Cadiz, Dumanoir realized that the battle was lost. He and his four ships steered south-east, first for the Straits of Gibraltar and later for Rochefort. This marked the end of any prospect of a turn in the Allies' fortunes through the intervention of the van squadron.

Elsewhere, resistance amongst many French and Spanish crews was collapsing. At 2.15pm, having fought with the *Royal Sovereign* for two

Evening of Trafalgar. British losses numbered over 1,000 killed and wounded, with Spanish casualties more than double that number. Perhaps 3,000 French died and over 1,000 were wounded. About 7,000 French and Spanish were captured. (National Maritime Museum, Greenwich: BHC 0542)

hours, the *Santa Ana* struck. Commodore Churruca of the *San Juan Nepomuceno*, under fire from six enemy ships, was struck by a cannon shot which nearly severed his right leg. 'It is nothing,' he called out as he propped himself up by his elbow. 'Go on firing.' Taken below and bleeding profusely, he directed the ensign to be nailed to the mast. Morale broke at news of the commander's death, and, with a third of the ship's company *hors de combat*, all her masts gone and her rudder smashed, the crew struck her colours.

Other Allied vessels were in similarly dire straits. Aboard the *Intrépide*, Captain Louis Infernet had lost half his crew; his masts had all been shot away and his hold filled with eight feet of water. The *Intrépide* had sought to assist the *Redoutable* in what one of her crew later described as 'a reckless and forlorn hope, a mad enterprise. It was a noble madness, but, though we knew it, we all supported him [Infernet] with joyful alacrity – and would that others had imitated his example!' Amidst this maelstrom, with heaps of dead and wounded around him, Infernet stood on the poop brandishing his curved sabre, stubbornly refusing to yield. 'But', recorded Gicquel des Touches, 'by now the decks had been almost swept clear, our guns were disabled, and the batteries heaped with dead and dying. It was impossible to keep up a resistance which meant the doom of what remained of our brave ship's company.' Infernet's officers, seeing that further exertion would be futile and could only result in needless additional losses, had to restrain their captain from behind while the colours were lowered.

GUN CREWS IN ACTION ON THE MIDDLE DECK OF THE VICTORY (74–75)

Gun crews in action on the middle deck of the *Victory* working feverishly to deliver broadsides against the enemy. However ponderous and slow-moving, ships of the line were extremely powerful floating fortresses. The *Victory*'s three tiers of guns – fifty on each side, plus carronades – could throw a broadside weight of approximately half a ton of metal about a mile and a half. Billowing smoke, the deafening thunder of the guns discharging and recoiling, the shouts of the officers and the cries of the wounded all combined to create a hellish atmosphere. A gun crew (1) manhandles a 24-pdr (so-called because of the weight of the shot it fired) back into position with the aid of hand-spikes. Guns were mounted on wheeled carriages so that when they were fired the breech ropes and side tackles could absorb the violent recoil. A gun captain pulls the lanyard (2), setting off the flintlock and igniting the charge. A veteran gun crew could reload, aim and fire their weapon every 90 seconds. A barrel of hand weapons (3) contains cutlasses, boarding axes and loaded pistols, ready for boarders or for repelling enemy boarders. A gunner (4) selects a round shot from an ammunition rack. This standard form of projectile consisted of a solid iron sphere weighing 12, 18, 24 or 32 pounds, depending on the size of the gun used to fire it. At short range, round shot had a devastating effect on the enemy's hull and masts. Gunners pull on the tackles (5) as they prepare to run out a gun. As all guns were muzzle-loaders they had to be rolled inboard for loading and then rolled out so that the barrel protruded through the gun port when ready to fire. At the breech the gun captain (6) will pierce the flannel cartridge before the charge is primed with gunpowder and the weapon fired. A powder monkey (7) scurries back to the magazine, clutching a canister that held a cartridge containing up to 11 pounds of black powder. The deck (8) is strewn with sand to aid in traction and to soak up blood and sea water. The men go barefoot to prevent their slipping as the ship pitches and rolls. A lieutenant (9), sword in hand, encourages the men, while the midshipman on the left awaits orders. Cannon, or 'great guns' as they were officially known, ranged in size depending on the class of ship that carried them and were known by the size of the round shot they discharged. Ships of the line carried between 74 and 120 guns, varying in calibre. A 32-pdr, crewed by up to a dozen men, could propel a shot to a maximum range of 2,000 yards. An 18- or 24-pounder could fire a shot as far as 3,000 yards, depending in each case on the amount of powder used in the charge and the elevation of the gun. The 12-pdr, the standard weapon of frigates, had a maximum range of approximately 1,800 yards, as did the 9-pounder. The effectiveness of round shot in penetrating a ship's hull depended principally on the range to the target, but also on the weight of the charge. When, as they often did, ships approached to very short distances – such as 30 yards – an 18-pound shot could penetrate 32 inches of oak planking and propel the resulting storm of splinters as far as thirty yards. At ten times that distance – 300 yards – even grape shot fired from a 32-pdr caused considerable damage, passing through five inches of fir planks or four inches of oak. In short, the destructive power of naval guns, particularly of the higher calibres and at short range, was considerable indeed. (Christa Hook)

By mid-afternoon the *Redoutable* was a shattered hulk, bereft of her main and mizzen masts, with the wreckage of the *Téméraire*'s top yards straddling her deck. Her poop was ruined, her helm, tiller, rudder and stern post were smashed, her stern was in flames, her decks shot through and her deck beams shattered. Most of her guns had been dismounted or rendered otherwise useless, the bulk of her crew had become casualties and four of her six pumps were disabled and water was rising in the hold. 'In the midst of this horrible carnage and devastation,' Lucas later recalled, 'my splendid fellows who had not been killed, and even, too, the wounded below on the orlop, kept cheering, "Long live the Emperor! We are not taken yet! Is the Captain still alive?"' He was alive, but, no longer willing to sacrifice his men to no further purpose, he finally surrendered his ship; the *Swiftsure* proceeded to take her in tow.

The end of the battle could be said to have been symbolically played out through the tragedy of the French ship, *Achille*. By mid-afternoon she had lost hundreds of her crew killed and wounded, including all of her senior officers. While engaged with the *Prince*, 98, her fore top caught fire, igniting other sails and spars. The crew tried to cut down the fore mast and push the blazing wreckage over the side, but when a subsequent broadside from the *Prince* brought her main mast – also ablaze – crashing down on the deck, the flames spread rapidly, quickly moving below. The *Prince* ceased fire, cleared away from her opponent to avoid catastrophe to herself, and then lowered boats into the water in an effort to rescue the French sailors abandoning ship.

At 5.45pm, when the flames reached the magazine, the *Achille* blew up. 'It was a sight the most awful and grand that can be conceived,' an officer aboard the *Defence*, 74, later recalled.

> *In a moment the hull burst into a cloud of smoke and fire. A column of vivid flame shot up to an enormous height in the atmosphere and terminated by expanding into an immense globe, representing for a few seconds, a prodigious tree in flames, specked with many dark spots, which the pieces of timber and bodies of men occasioned while they were suspended in the clouds.*

Out of her original 499-man complement only about 100 sailors were plucked out of the water by British ships in the vicinity.

Firing gradually faded away after this horrific episode in what had been a ferocious day's fighting. The British fleet had convincingly beaten its opponents, capturing or destroying 18 of the 33 ships of the Combined Fleet, representing a loss of 55 per cent of their force. This achievement was the result of careful planning as well as hard fighting, as Collingwood explained after the battle: 'A Victory, the effect of system and nice combination, not of chance.' None of the British ships was lost, though many had suffered extreme damage, and losses were heavy on both sides. Modern historians suggest Spanish losses of 1,038 killed or drowned and 1,385 wounded, including Gravina. Although there are no official French records, the best estimates are approximately 3,370 killed or drowned and more than 1,160 wounded. Twenty-six of the flag officers and captains of the Combined Fleet were killed or wounded, and approximately 7,000 French and Spanish became prisoners, including Villeneuve himself, representing a loss of almost one in four.

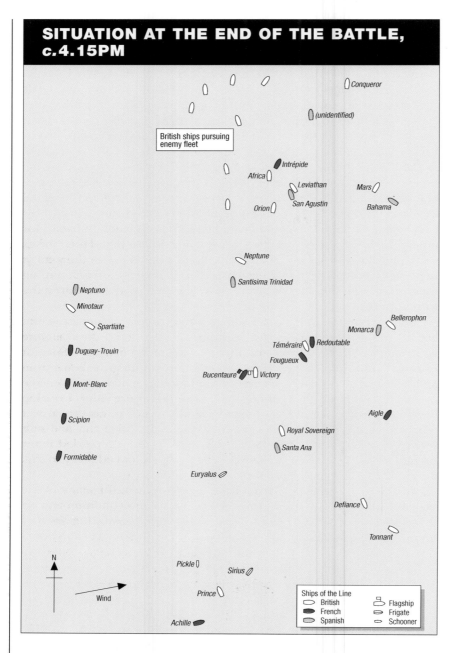

Conqueror

(unidentified)

British ships pursuing enemy fleet

Intrépide

Africa

Leviathan

Mars

San Agustin

Bahama

Orion

Neptune

Neptuno

Santisima Trinidad

Minotaur

Spartiate

Bellerophon

Monarca

Duguay-Trouin

Téméraire   Redoutable

Fougueux

Mont-Blanc

Bucentaure   Victory

Scipion

Aigle

Royal Sovereign

Formidable

Santa Ana

Euryalus

Defiance

Tonnant

N

Pickle

Sirius

Prince

Wind

Achille

Ships of the Line
British
French
Spanish
Flagship
Frigate
Schooner

British losses were remarkably small: 449 officers and men killed (including Captains Duff and Cooke) and 1,214 wounded, or approximately 10 per cent of the total force. The greatest loss for the British, of course, was that of their revered admiral, who had saved the nation through brilliant leadership and bold fighting tactics. The men wept openly at his loss for, as William Robinson related in his memoirs, '... he was adored, and in fighting under him, every man thought himself sure of success.'

AFTERMATH

BRAVING THE STORM

Despite Nelson's last order, 'Anchor, Hardy, Anchor!' Collingwood unaccountably did not do so, perhaps because too many of his vessels were incapable of carrying out the task. In any event, for most of the following week men aboard the British ships and their prizes desperately struggled to survive. There was no time to savour the victory: the crews now had to battle the elements for their very survival, putting their vessels in a seaworthy state as the swells grew higher and the gales gathered momentum.

Urgent and extensive repairs were essential, for a hurricane was brewing in the Atlantic, and by the evening of the 22nd the seas were churning so hard that aboard the prizes the French and Spanish prisoners were released in order to assist in preventing the ships from foundering. This created an extraordinary spectacle: men who, only the previous day had been killing one another, were now exerting themselves for their mutual survival. Damaged rigging was thrust over the side and shot holes stopped up. Those ships which still had sails sought to tow those that did not. Prize money to be rewarded many British sailors evaporated as many captured vessels looked likely to sink or crash into the rocky Spanish coast.

The storm could not have struck at a worse time, for many of the vessels were virtual wrecks. The *Redoutable*, her pitiful condition already described, was leaking badly, and had been taken in tow by the *Swiftsure* on the day of the battle, but by noon on the 22nd it was clear she would sink and boats were sent to take off the wounded. Nevertheless, only 119

HMS *Swiftsure* rescuing the crew of the *Redoutable*. Severe leaking aboard the French prize necessitated urgent assistance from British ships. Nevertheless, only 119 of her crew were saved before 10pm, when the *Redoutable* sank with practically all her wounded still on board. (PH 10296: 'Combat de Trafalgar. Le *Redoutable* coulant à fond à la remorque du Swift-Sure.' © Musée national de la marine, Paris)

were saved and when at about 10pm, the great ship slipped beneath the surface, most of her wounded went with her. Only 169 of her ship's company. survived the battle, some of them rescued from floating wreckage on the 23rd.

The *Belleisle*, reduced to nothing more than a smoking, riddled hulk, was towed by the frigate *Naiad*, 38, bound for Gibraltar. Jury masts were improvised by her exhausted crew, her pumps working continuously, and by the afternoon of the 22nd some of her fore and aft sails could be set. The log of the *Agamemnon* the day after the battle noted the ship making three feet of water per hour, and she had the stricken *Colossus*, 74, in tow.

The *Fougueux* ran ashore and was wrecked, as was the *Monarca* which, while being towed towards Gibraltar by the *Donegal*, 74 (which had not been present at Trafalgar), broke free of the towing cable and was dashed against a rocky shore, causing the death of her entire ship's company as well as the 30 men of *Téméraire*'s prize crew. Aboard the *Algésiras* the prisoners were released by the 50-man prize crew of the *Tonnant* to help steer the dismasted vessel into Cadiz. They succeeded, but the prize crew then themselves became prisoners.

For the wounded, the gale was a nightmare as the ships rolled and swayed, heeled and plunged amidst heavy seas. Many succumbed to their wounds when they might otherwise have survived the ordeal. Aboard the *Fougueux*, Pierre Servaux noted how, as the water rose nearly to the orlop deck, 'Everywhere one heard the cries of the wounded and the dying, as well as the noise and shouts of insubordinate men who refused to man the pumps and only thought of themselves.'

Aboard the captured Spanish 74 *Monarca*, a midshipman from the *Bellerophon*, which had dispatched a prize crew, recalled the utter sense of exhaustion and despair which pervaded the ship:

> *I felt not the least fear of death during the action: but in the prize, when I had time to reflect upon the approach of death, I was most certainly afraid, and at one time, when the ship made three feet of water in ten minutes, when our people were almost all lying drunk upon deck, when the Spaniards, completely worn out with fatigue, would no longer work at the only chain pump left serviceable, I wrapped myself up in a Union Jack and lay down upon deck.*

The *Santísima Trinidad* was a giant dismasted wreck. She remained floating for almost three days, while crews from the British vessels *Ajax* and *Revenge* flung her dead overboard and removed her wounded into boats rocking in the water below. 'Tis impossible to describe the horrors the morning presented', Lieutenant John Edwards of the *Prince*, 98, later wrote.

> *Nothing but signals of distress flying in every direction. The signal was made to destroy the prizes. We had no time before to remove the prisoners; but what a sight when we came to remove the wounded, of which there were between three and four hundred. We had to tie the poor mangled wretches round their waists, and lower them down into a tumbling boat, some without arms, others no legs, and lacerated all over in the most dreadful manner.*

Less than half the four-decker's crew of 1,115 were saved. On the 24th, amid severe winds, her towing hawsers broke twice. The once-mighty ship was abandoned, with some of her most severely wounded still on board. 'A dull roar of terror echoed through the ship', Perez Galdos recalled. 'Up through the hatchways came a hideous shriek. It came from the poor wretches on the lower deck, who already felt the waters rising to drown them and vainly cried for help to God or men.'

Collingwood later wrote to the Admiralty of his grave fears for the safety of his fleet while his own flagship was under tow:

The condition of our own ships was such that it was very doubtful what would be their fate. Many a time I would have given the whole group of our capture, to ensure our own ... I can only say that in my life I never saw such efforts as were made to save these ships, and would rather fight another battle than pass through such a week as followed it.

The other flagship, the *Victory*, bearing Nelson's body, entered Gibraltar safely on the 28th, towed in by the *Neptune*.

The storm was not the only threat encountered by the fleet in the wake of Trafalgar. Commodore Baron Cosmao-Kerjulien had replaced the captive Villeneuve and mortally wounded Gravina; he hoped to recapture some of the prizes off Cadiz while their prisoners and prize crews struggled to raise jury rigs and avoid crashing against a lee shore. On the 24th Cosmao-Kerjulien sortied from Cadiz, causing Collingwood reluctantly to order the prizes scuttled and burnt. The *Conqueror*, towing the *Bucentaure*, containing prisoners and a prize crew, abandoned the former Allied flagship, which then drifted ashore. Some of the men were rescued by sailors from two other captured French ships.

With the French ships of the line *Pluton*, 74, *Indomptable*, 80, and *Neptune*, 84, and the Spanish *Rayo*, 100, and *San Francisco de Asís*, 74, together with five French frigates and two brigs, Cosmao-Kerjulien confronted about ten British ships. These, being the least damaged, formed line of battle, interposing themselves between the attackers and the crippled prizes. Cosmoa declined to attack this force, but his frigates isolated and recaptured two of the prizes, the *Neptuno* and the *Santa Ana*. These recovered vessels made it back to Cadiz under tow; the other Allied prizes under tow by British frigates were blown towards the Spanish coast and had to be abandoned owing to worsening weather.

On balance, the Allied counter-attack achieved little. In forcing the British to suspend their repairs in order to defend themselves, it probably influenced Collingwood's decision to sink or set fire to the most damaged of his remaining prizes. Cosmao retook two Spanish ships of the line, but it cost him one French and two Spanish vessels to do so. Despite his loss, the action was a daring gesture on the part of Allies who, despite their decisive defeat only days before, were prepared to face their enemy, albeit weakened, on another occasion.

More tragedy awaited the survivors of Trafalgar. The day after Cosmao's sortie the *Indomptable*, having been grounded, broke apart with over 1,000 men on board, many of them survivors of the *Bucentaure*. Only a tenth of the men reached the shore safely. The *San Francisco de Asís* beached itself in Cadiz Bay and the *Rayo*, which had anchored and had to throw overboard her masts, was captured by the *Donegal*, fresh from Gibraltar. Yet even this prize was lost when she was grounded and wrecked on the 26th. The *Bucentaure*, mastless and battered, washed up on the shore near the entrance to Cadiz harbour, where her British prize crew was taken prisoner, but treated with courtesy. Other prize crews driven ashore were well received, their wounds dressed and their thirst and appetites satisfied. In the end, only four prizes remained in British possession – one French and three Spanish.

The last encounter of the campaign took place on 2 November, when a squadron under Sir Richard Strachan, consisting of the *Caesar*, 80, and three 74s, the *Hero*, *Courageux* and *Namur*, took on the remnant of the enemy van from Trafalgar that had escaped southward under Dumanoir Le Pelley. Strachan found him in the Bay of Biscay in the latitude of Cape Finisterre, the enemy force consisting of Dumanoir's flagship the *Formidable*, 80, and three 74s: the *Duguay-Trouin*, *Mont-Blanc* and *Scipion*. The British captured all four French vessels and carried them back to Plymouth, where they eventually saw service in the Royal Navy, two of them under new names. Strachan's remarkable achievement cost him only 24 killed and 111 wounded, whereas he inflicted an astonishing 750 killed and wounded on the enemy.

Meanwhile, at Cadiz, most of the Spanish vessels which had followed Gravina had reached this port safely, but in one of the campaign's great ironies the Spanish admiral, having survived the battle itself, died through the neglect of his doctors, who failed to amputate his arm before gangrene set in. Nothing then could be done to save him, or the many others similarly wounded. Indeed, the scene at Cadiz was horrendous. A British merchant there noted that even ten days after the battle, residents were still busy carrying survivors ashore:

The wounded were carried away to the hospitals in every shape of human misery, whilst crowds of Spaniards either assisted or looked on with signs of horror. Meanwhile, their companions, who had escaped unhurt, walked up and down with folded arms and downcast eyes ... As

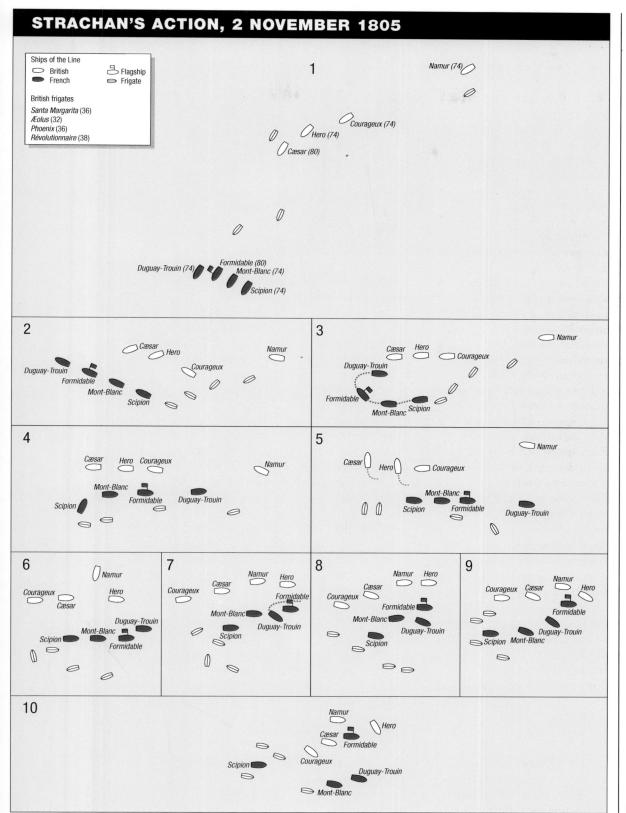

Strachan's action. A postscript to Trafalgar in which Sir Richard Strachan pursued the four ships under Dumanoir Le Pelley which had escaped southwards after the great battle. Both sides were evenly matched, yet Strachan captured every enemy vessel and inflicted 750 casualties. (National Maritime Museum, Greenwich: PAD 5757)

far as the eye could reach, the sandy side of the isthmus bordering on the Atlantic was covered with masts and yards, the wrecks of ships, and here and there the bodies of the dead.

Such scenes greeted Admiral Rosily, the Emperor's replacement for Villeneuve, when he arrived at Cadiz on 25 October with the task of reporting the defeat of the Combined Fleet, directing rescue operations and sending burial parties to the beaches where the tide continued to deposit bodies on the sand for days after the guns had fallen silent.

With the battle over and Nelson dead, the task of reporting the victory fell to Collingwood who, having transferred his flag to the frigate *Euryalus*, wrote a dispatch to the Admiralty the day after the action. This was conveyed to England by Lieutenant Lapenotière in the schooner *Pickle*, 10, who landed at Falmouth on 5 November and raced by successive fresh horses to the Admiralty in Whitehall where he arrived, breathless, at 1.30am on the morning of the 6th. William Marsden, the First Secretary of the Admiralty, awoke Lord Barham. 'Sir', he said, 'we have gained a great victory, but we have lost Lord Nelson.' Clerks soon began making copies of Collingwood's dispatch, bearing news of the loss of the commander-in-chief and containing a brief account of the battle, for Pitt, the king, and for the *London Gazette*.

Collingwood's dispatch stands as one of the great documents of British naval history. Eloquent, moving, though at times factually inaccurate, it revealed the great personal loss the author felt for his fallen superior. Having briefly described the events which preceded the battle, Collingwood went on to describe the action itself, and closed with a heartfelt passage:

After such a Victory, it may appear unnecessary to enter into enconiums on the particular parts taken by the several Commanders; the conclusion says more on the subject than I have language to express; the spirit which animated all was the same: when all exert themselves zealously in the country's service, all deserve that their high merit should stand recorded; and never was high merit more conspicuous than in the battle I have described.

On Nelson himself, Collingwood continued:

Such a battle could not be fought without sustaining a great loss of men. I have not only to lament, in common with the British Navy, and the British Nation, in the Fall of the Commander in Chief, the loss of a Hero, whose name will be immortal, and his memory ever dear to his country; but my heart is rent with the most poignant grief for the death of a friend, to whom, by many years' intimacy, and a perfect knowledge of the virtues of his mind, which supplied ideas superior to the common race of men, I was bound by the strongest ties of affection, a grief to which even the glorious occasion in which he fell, does not bring the consolation which, perhaps it ought …

Captain Blackwood of the *Euryalus* and a friend of Nelson's, wrote to his wife the day after the battle:

My heart … is sad, and penetrated with the deepest anguish. A Victory, such a one as has never been achieved, yesterday took place in the course of five hours; but at such an expense, in the loss of the most gallant of men, and best of friends, as renders it to me a Victory I never wished to have witnessed – at least, on such terms … Lord Nelson … has left cause for every man who had a heart never to forget him … the Fleet [at Trafalgar] under any other [commander], never would have performed what they did under Lord N. But under Lord N. it seemed like inspiration to most of them.

Despite the loss of her greatest admiral, Britain sorely needed such a victory, for only days before word had arrived that Napoleon, during his march to the Danube, had surrounded and captured an army of 30,000 Austrians at Ulm. On 2 December, the French Emperor followed up this victory with a decisive defeat over the Austro-Russian army at Austerlitz, in Moravia, which knocked the Austrians out of the war and obliged Tsar Alexander to retreat east with his army. The Third Coalition lay in tatters. Yet Napoleon, master though he was on land, remained confined to it, thanks to Nelson.

The mortal remains of the fallen hero could hardly be consigned to the sea as was common practice for the disposal of the dead. On the contrary, the country would have its saviour returned to home soil where, when news of his death arrived, the whole nation mourned. His friend, Lord Minto, wrote:

> *We shall want more victories yet, and to whom can we look for them? The navy is certainly full of the bravest men, but … brave as they almost all are, there was a sort of heroic cast about Nelson that I never saw in any other man, and which seems wanting to the achievement of <u>impossible things</u> which became easy to him…*

Dr Beatty, the *Victory*'s surgeon, undertook the task of preserving Nelson's body, a procedure that involved placing the remains in a cask filled with brandy and lashed to the main mast on the middle deck, guarded day and night by a sentry. On the third night the guard nearly ran off in fright when an exhalation of gas from the body forced the lid of the cask to rise. The wounded were sent ashore at Gibraltar on 28 October and a week later the *Victory* proceeded back through the Straits to rejoin the fleet, which then sailed back to England through rough seas.

On reaching the Nore, off Portsmouth, on 23 December, the *Victory* gave over Nelson's coffin, covered in an ensign, to the Admiralty Commissioners' yacht which then conveyed it to Greenwich. There the body lay in state for three days in the Painted Hall at Greenwich Hospital, attracting as many as 100,000 mourners who slowly filed past, until on 8 January, in the midst of a hard south-westerly wind, Nelson's coffin – the one fashioned from the main mast of *L'Orient* – was brought up-river to the Admiralty in the midst of a procession of hundreds of boats stretching two miles. Early on the morning of the 9th, the coffin was placed on a specially-constructed bier and slowly pulled through the streets of London to St Paul's Cathedral in a massive funeral procession consisting of ministers, noblemen, members of the royal family, 32 admirals, more than a hundred captains and an army of other mourners in train. Thousands of people lined the streets in silent observance. After a lengthy service the coffin, lowered into the crypt by a party of sailors from the *Victory*, came to rest in a magnificent sarcophagus originally intended for Henry VIII's chancellor, Cardinal Wolsey.

It will be recalled that on the morning of the battle Nelson had written a codicil to his will in which he had requested provision for Lady Hamilton and their daughter. These requests were ignored, for neither the government nor Parliament would contemplate publicly admitting

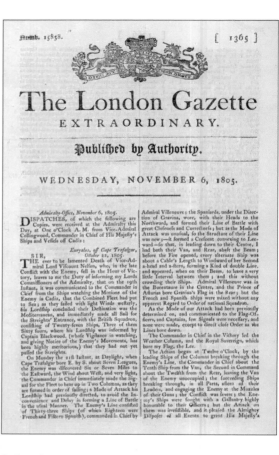

London Gazette announcing the outcome of battle. Once the Admiralty revealed the contents of Collingwood's despatch, newspapers throughout the capital printed multiple editions containing the details of the fighting and, later, lists of casualties. (Royal Naval Museum, Portsmouth)

Victory towed into Gibraltar by HMS *Neptune*, 28 October 1805. The preservation of Nelson's flagship, not to mention the vice-admiral's body itself, was of enormous psychological importance. Damage sustained in battle had been severe: *Victory*'s mizzen mast was shot away, the main yard gone, the fore and main tops damaged, and the fore yard and main topsail yard torn away. (Royal Naval Museum, Portsmouth)

Nelson's body lying in state in the Painted Hall at Greenwich Hospital. So intense was the outpouring of public grief that the government decided to accord the nation's hero a state funeral. (Royal Naval Museum, Portsmouth)

ABOVE **Nelson's funeral cortège arriving at St Paul's. The procession was so long that the head of the column reached the cathedral before the tail had even left the Admiralty in Whitehall. (Royal Naval Museum, Portsmouth)**

LEFT **Interment of Nelson in St Paul's Cathedral, 9 January 1806. The Vice-Admiral's state funeral ranks as one of the most lavish in British history. Hundreds watched solemnly in tiers of seats as his coffin was lowered into the crypt below. Captured French and Spanish flags adorn the walls. (Royal Naval Museum, Portsmouth)**

the connection between Nelson and his mistress, nor of his obviously illegitimate daughter. Emma Hamilton did not, however, go without provision, for both Nelson and the late Sir William Hamilton left her substantial sums of money. Extravagance and squandering habits nevertheless led her to flee to Calais to avoid imprisonment for debt, and she died there penniless in 1815. Horatia was adopted by Nelson's younger sister and later married a rector, Philip Ward. She died in 1881.

SIGNIFICANCE OF THE BATTLE

The battle had important consequences in both the short and the long term. Within three months of Trafalgar British troops were ensconced on Sicily, securing that island as a permanent British station for the remainder of the Napoleonic Wars. With Malta also in British hands, and with the Mediterranean under the control of the Royal Navy, French expansion into the eastern Mediterranean was considerably less likely than ever before. The French fleet was unable to pose any significant threat for the remainder of the Napoleonic Wars. Having defeated France decisively, Britain was enabled to assume the offensive in the struggle against Napoleon, making it possible only three years after Trafalgar for her to land troops and supplies in the Iberian Peninsula, so opening a new front against the French Empire. The Peninsular campaigns, led by the Duke of Wellington, would place heavy demands on the French army between 1808 and 1814, whereas conversely, British command of the sea enabled Wellington to receive reinforcements and supplies completely unmolested. In short, Trafalgar confined Napoleonic rule to the Continent, and at the same time enabled Britain to oppose France in what would become, by 1812, a major theatre of conflict on land.

In the longer term, Trafalgar stands as the most decisive naval battle of modern times. It marked both the beginning and the end of an era: the beginning of over a century of British naval mastery, and the end of fleet actions fought under sail, as well as to two centuries of maritime rivalry between Britain, France and Spain. Nelson's objective – to destroy the Franco-Spanish fleet in order to eliminate the threat of invasion to the British Isles – had been achieved, and with overwhelming success. For a hundred years after the Napoleonic Wars, Britain's control of the seas was unassailable. The battle came at a time when the Industrial Revolution was gaining momentum; with Britain undisputed mistress of the seas, the nation was assured of raw materials for export and home consumption, and of food for a population too large to be fed by domestic production. The routes to markets overseas remained uncontested, and the foundations were laid for imperial expansion on a scale not seen since the height of the Roman Empire.

THE BATTLEFIELD TODAY

SURVIVING RELICS AND RECORDS

By the very nature of a battle fought in the open sea about 27 miles south-south-east of Cadiz and 40 miles west of Gibraltar, nothing remains for the curious to see in terms of landmarks. However, some of the relics of the battle, and of Nelson in particular, remain, above all the splendidly restored *Victory* herself, which since 1922 has sat in No 2 Dock off the basin in the Portsmouth Historic Dockyard, Hampshire. She is open to the public, draws 360,000 visitors annually, and is easily accessible by train to Portsmouth Harbour station. Marked on the quarter deck is the spot where Nelson fell, as is the place on the orlop deck where he died. Some of his original furniture remains in his cabin. In addition to the books listed in the bibliography below, the Royal Navy maintains an official website (www.hms-victory.com) that provides facts and statistics about the ship.

The Royal Naval Museum, now housed in the 18th-century storehouses at Portsmouth, holds numerous items connected with Nelson and Trafalgar in its Victory Gallery. Visitors can access 'The Ayshford Trafalgar Roll', an exhaustive database providing the names and other information of all the men present at the battle on the British side. This is complemented by access to 'The Complete Navy List of the Napoleonic Wars', which contains similar information on British naval officers in the period 1793–1815.

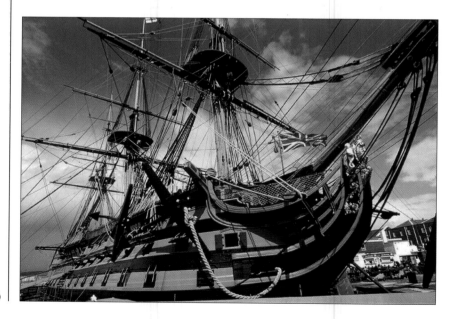

HMS *Victory* in dry dock, fully restored and fitted out exactly as she appeared in 1805. Nelson's flagship and the Royal Naval Museum opposite are an essential stop for anyone pursuing an interest in the 'age of fighting sail' in general, and the battle of Trafalgar in particular. (POA (Phot) Gary Davies)

Trafalgar Cemetary, Gibraltar: the gravestone of a British sailor who succumbed to wounds received at Trafalgar, but who survived long enough to reach land. Such graves are rare: the bodies of those killed at sea were almost invariably cast overboard, usually unceremoniously, Nelson and other senior officers excepted. (Travelpictures.co.uk)

Many objects and sites associated with the battle may be found in London. The National Maritime Museum at Greenwich (best reached by boat down the Thames from Westminster Pier, but also accessible by car or bus), has preserved many Nelsonian relics, including the coat, breeches and stockings worn by the vice-admiral during the battle. The hole produced by the musket ball that killed him can be clearly seen on the left shoulder of the coat, while the stockings are still stained with his blood. An entire gallery is dedicated to Nelson and his exploits, including numerous paintings, prints and engravings of Trafalgar. The museum also houses invaluable archival material, many portraits of Nelson and his officers, and a variety of other paintings and objects associated not only with the Trafalgar campaign, but with Britain's naval conflict with France during the period 1793–1815.

The Royal Naval College, formerly the Royal Hospital for Seamen, stands across the road from the Maritime Museum. It was in its Painted Hall that Nelson lay in state before being transported up the Thames to Whitehall steps.

Trafalgar Square in London remains a major landmark of the capital, with Nelson's Column the highlight of this Victorian triumph. The four lions which sit at its base were cast from iron cannon captured at Trafalgar. The National Portrait Gallery, off Trafalgar Square, contains pictures of Nelson and some of his captains present at the battle.

The National Archives (formerly the Public Record Office) at Kew in west London is easily accessible by Underground, and holds a vast collection of official manuscripts connected with the Trafalgar campaign, including the Admiralty Papers (ADM) which contain communications between the Admiralty and the various station commanders, together with many ships' muster rolls and captains' logs. Numerous correspondence and documents connected with the campaign may, however, be more easily consulted in volumes VI and VII of *The Dispatches and Letters of Lord Nelson*, originally edited by Sir Nicholas Harris Nicolas between 1844 and 1847 but now recently reprinted. The British Library, in central London, holds valuable correspondence sent to Nelson in the final months of the campaign in Add. Mss 34931. Numerous other valuable collections may be identified in the bibliographies of recent monographs on the campaign.

Nelson's impressive tomb is well worth a visit and can be seen in the crypt of St Paul's Cathedral, directly beneath the dome.

Beyond Portsmouth and London, the Nelson Museum in Priory Street, Monmouth is of interest. The village of Burnham Thorpe, in Norfolk, where Nelson was born and spent his childhood, is quiet and picturesque, and while his father's original rectory has long since been demolished, the church of All Saints in which Edmund Nelson preached still stands. The graves of various members of the Nelson family can be found in the churchyard. Chatham Historic Dockyard, in Kent, contains many buildings and exhibits connected with the age of sail, including the site of the Old Single Dock where the *Victory* was constructed between 1759 and 1765. Buckler's Hard, an 18th-century Hampshire village on the banks of the Beaulieu River in the New Forest, contains a maritime museum which houses pictures, models and artefacts pertaining to the construction of Royal Navy vessels built near the site during Nelson's time.

Further afield, in Gibraltar, the graves of two men who were brought ashore after the battle and subsequently died of their wounds may be seen in the Trafalgar Cemetery, which lies at the end of Main Street near the cable car station at Grand Parade. Formerly known as Southport Ditch Cemetery and dating from 1798, the cemetery also holds the graves of victims of a yellow fever epidemic and of other Anglo-French naval actions of the period.

Much of Cadiz, which stands on an island, looks as it did in 1805, with its low white houses and narrow streets radiating out from the Tavira Tower, the tallest mirador in the city. From the top of it, looking south, can be seen long, sandy beaches, which eventually give way to the rocky shoals of Cape Trafalgar. To the south-east of the city is the Isla de Léon, off which Villeneuve's fleet lay at anchor prior to the battle.

The many works still produced on Nelson the man and his campaigns bear testament to his hold over the British imagination. Despite a proper revision of the contemporary idolization of Nelson, historians continue to find his character and career compelling. The last word might be left to the poet Samuel Taylor Coleridge, who after the commander's death wrote:

Lord Nelson was an admiral every inch of him. He looked at everything, not merely in its possible relations to the naval service in general, but in its immediate bearings on his own squadron; to his officers, his men, to the particular ships themselves, his affections were as strong and ardent as those of a lover ... never was a commander so enthusiastically loved by men of all ranks, from the captain of the fleet to the youngest ship-boy.

GLOSSARY OF NAVAL TERMS

The terminology associated with ships and the sea is very large and can fill an entire book. Below are some of the technical terms referred to in this work, as well as others that may interest the reader.

Aft To the rear of the vessel, e.g. 'to go aft'.

Aloft Up in the masts or rigging.

Astern Behind the vessel.

Boarding Coming aboard an enemy vessel by force.

Boom off To push a vessel off with a pole.

Bow The forward (front-most) part of a vessel.

Brig A lightly-armed (c.14 guns), manoeuvrable, square-rigged, two-masted vessel, smaller than a sloop.

Broadside The simultaneous firing of all the guns positioned on one side of the ship.

Bulwark The side of a ship from the deck to the gunwale.

Canister shot A type of ammunition consisting of a cylindrical tin case packed with many iron balls which when fired from a cannon at short range spread out to kill and maim enemy personnel.

Carronade A short-barrelled, heavy-calibre gun used only at close range for devastating results against the enemy's hull and crew. Only the Royal Navy carried such weapons, which were not counted in the rating of vessel.

Chain shot A type of ammunition comprised of two iron spheres or half-spheres, connected by a short length of chain, mainly used to damage masts, rigging and sails.

Cockpit The rear section of the orlop deck, usually the quarters of the midshipmen and others, but used for the treatment of the wounded in action.

Flagship The ship of the officer commanding a squadron or fleet, usually a vice- or rear-admiral, and flying his flag.

Fleet A force of more than ten warships.

Flotilla A force of small vessels, sometimes troop ships and gun boats.

Fore To the front of the vessel.

Forecastle Short deck positioned at the front of the ship.

Frigate A single-decked warship mounting between 24 and 44 guns.

Gaff A type of short spar.

Gangway Narrow platform connecting the quarter deck with the fore-castle.

Grape shot A type of ammunition consisting of a canvas bag filled with small iron balls, which when fired from a cannon spread out to kill and maim enemy personnel.

Gun A cannon. These fired round shot weighing between 12 and 36 pounds. Small arms, technically speaking, were not 'guns', but referred to by their specific type, e.g. musket, pistol, etc.

Gun deck A deck on which is mounted a battery of guns.

Gunwale Timbers running along the tops of bulwarks.

Jury rig An improvised device used to sail a damaged (e.g. a dismasted) vessel pending permanent repair, usually at the nearest port.

Landsman A man with no naval training and therefore incapable, at least initially, of performing anything beyond unskilled tasks, such as hauling and hoisting.

Langridge A type of shot consisting of jagged pieces of iron which when fired spread out to damage rigging and sails and to kill men on the upper deck.

Lanyard A short length of rope which when pulled engaged the firing mechanism and discharged a gun.

Larboard The left-hand (port) side of the vessel as one looks forward towards the bow.

Lee The side of a vessel opposite to that from which the wind is blowing. A ship 'to leeward' was one downwind.

Lee shore A shore towards which the wind is blowing a vessel.

Leeward In the direction towards which the wind is blowing.

Line of battle The positioning of warships in a line with their broadsides facing an enemy against whom they intend to engage in battle.

Luff To steer or sail more toward the direction from which the wind is blowing.

Masts The vertical spars, all of which carried sails, yards, gaffs and smaller, horizontal spars. All ships had three masts: the main (tallest, in the centre, which supported the principal sails), the fore (towards the front of the vessel) and the mizzen (to the rear of the vessel).

Nautical mile One nautical mile equals 6,080 feet.

Orlop deck The lowest deck on a large vessel, at or below the waterline, where the cockpit was situated.

Poop A short deck situated above the quarter deck deck at the rear of the vessel.

Port The left-hand side of a ship when looking toward the bow. Opposite of 'starboard'.

Prize A captured enemy vessel.

Prize money Money paid to officers and men, according to their respective ranks and the value of the captured vessel, upon sale to their own naval establishment.

Quarter deck The deck above the upper deck extending from the far end of the waist (the middle section of the ship) and above it to the stern. This was the part of the ship where the captain or officer of the watch commanded the ship.

Quoin A wooden wedge used to adjust the elevation of a gun.

Rate/Rating The classification of a warship according to the number of guns it carried. First rates carried the most, sixth rates the fewest.

Rake To fire at an enemy ship's bow or stern when it is at right angle to one's one vessel, so enabling the shot to travel down the length of the enemy ship.

Rigging Ropes used for two purposes: standing rigging supported the masts; running rigging was used to raise and lower sails, and to shift spars.

Ship In distinction from a boat, a square-rigged vessel with three masts.

Ship of the line Warship carrying a minimum of 64 guns that by virtue of its size and armament could fight in a line of battle; the standard type was the 74.

Shrouds Ropes used to support the masts of a ship which run from the mast to the ship's side.

Sloop A single-decked warship slightly smaller than a sixth-rate (frigate) but larger than a brig.

Spar A substantial pole or piece of timber from which sails are hung.

Squadron A group of fewer than ten ships.

Square-rigged A ship with supported horizontal square sails from its masts.

Stand on To hold a course.

Starboard The right-hand side of a vessel as one looks forward. Opposite of 'port'.

Stays Ropes used fore and aft that support the masts.

Stern The rear-most part of the hull, usually ornamented and especially vulnerable to enemy fire.

Strike (one's colours) To haul down the national flag to indicate a desire to surrender.

Top The platform fixed around the lower mast, primarily used by the men to work aloft, but also providing a place for look-outs and marksmen in battle.

Topgallant The highest of the three spars which, fitted together, comprise a mast.

Top hamper All the masts, rigging, spars and other features above the main deck.

Tumblehome The inward curve of a ship's upper sides which renders the upper deck narrower than the middle and lower decks (on a three-decked ship).

Van The leading vessels or squadron.

Weather To sail to windward of an object, such as a cape, an island or another feature.

Yard Spar suspended horizontally from a mast which holds up a square sail extended across the breadth of a ship.

BIBLIOGRAPHY

Adams, Max, *Trafalgar's Lost Hero: Admiral Lord Collingwood and the Defeat of Napoleon,* John Wiley & Sons Inc., London (2004)

Addis, C. P., *Men who fought with Nelson in HMS Victory at Trafalgar,* Nelson Society, London (1988)

Adkin, Mark, *The Trafalgar Companion: The Complete Guide to History's Most Famous Sea Battle and the Life of Admiral Lord Nelson,* Aurum Press, London (2005)

Adkins, Roy, *Trafalgar: The Biography of a Battle,* Little, Brown, London (2004)

Bennett, Geoffrey, *The Battle of Trafalgar,* Wharncliffe Books, London (2004)

_____, *Nelson the Commander,* Penguin, London (2002)

Best, Nicholas, *Trafalgar,* Weidenfeld & Nicolson, London (2005)

Bradford, Ernle, *Nelson: The Essential Hero,* Macmillan, London (1999)

Clayton, Tim and Craig, Phil, *Trafalgar,* Hodder & Stoughton Ltd., London (2004)

Clowes, William Laird, *The Royal Navy: A History from the Earliest Times to 1900,* vol. V, Chatham Publishing, London (1997)

Coleman, Terry, *Nelson: The Man and the Legend,* Bloomsbury, London (2002)

Corbett, Julian, *The Campaign of Trafalgar,* 2 vols., AMS Press, New York (1976)

Davies, Paul, *The Battle of Trafalgar,* Pan Books, London (1972)

Desbrière, Edouard, *The Naval Campaign of 1805: Trafalgar*, trans. and ed. by Constance Eastwick, 2 vols., Clarendon Press, Oxford (1933)

Fabb, John, and Cassin-Scott, Jack, *The Uniforms of Trafalgar,* Batsford, London (1977)

Fraser, Edward, Cznik, Marianne, and Nash, Michael, *The Enemy at Trafalgar: Eyewitness Narratives, Dispatches and Letters from the French and Spanish Fleets,* Chatham Publishing, London (2004)

Fremont-Barnes, Gregory, *Nelson's Sailors,* Osprey Publishing, Oxford (2005)

Gardiner, Robert, ed., *The Campaign of Trafalgar, 1803-1805,* Chatham Publishing, London (1997)

Glover, Richard, *Britain at Bay: Defence against Bonaparte, 1803-14,* Allen & Unwin, London (1973)

Goodwin, Peter, *Nelson's Victory: 101 Questions and Answers about HMS Victory, Nelson's Flagship at Trafalgar 1805,* Brassey's, London (2004)

_____, *The Ships of Trafalgar: The British, French and Spanish Fleets, 21 October 1805,* Conway Maritime Press, London (2005)

Harbron, John, *Trafalgar and the Spanish Navy: The Spanish Experience of Sea Power,* Conway Maritime Press, London (2004)

Hart, Roger, *England Expects,* Wayland Publishers, London (1972)

Hayward, Joel, *For God and Glory: Lord Nelson and His Way of War,* Naval Institute Press, Annapolis, MD (2003)

Howarth, David, *Trafalgar: The Nelson Touch,* Weidenfeld & Nicolson, London (2003)

Howarth, David, and Howarth, Stephen, *Nelson: The Immortal Memory,* S. M. Dent & Sons, London (1998)

Ireland, Bernard, *Naval Warfare in the Age of Sail,* Norton, New York (2000)

James, William, *The Naval History of Great Britain,* Vol IV, Conway Maritime Press, London (2002)

Lambert, Andrew, *Nelson: Britannia's God of War,* Faber & Faber Ltd., London (2004)

_____, *War at Sea in the Age of Sail,* Cassell, London (2000)

Langdon-Davies, John, ed. *Battle of Trafalgar: Collection of Contemporary Documents,* Jackdaw Publications (1963)

Lavery, Brian, *Nelson's Fleet at Trafalgar,* Naval Institute Press, Annapolis, MD (2004)

_____, *Nelson's Navy: The Ships, Men and Organisation, 1793-1815,* Conway Maritime Press, London (1989)

Legg, Stuart, *Trafalgar: An Eyewitness Account of a Great Battle,* Rupert Hart Davis, London (1966)

Leyland, John, ed., *Dispatches and Letters relating to the Blockade of Brest, 1803-1805,* 2 vols., Navy Records Society, London (1899, 1902)

Lyon, David, *Sea Battles in Close-up: The Age of Nelson,* Naval Institute Press, Annapolis, MD (1996)

Mackenzie, Robert Holden, *The Trafalgar Roll: The Officers, the Men, the Ships,* Chatham Publishing, London (2004)

Maine, René, *Trafalgar: Napoleon's Naval Waterloo,* Thames and Hudson, London (1957)

McGowan, Alan, *HMS Victory: Her Construction, Career and Restoration,* Chatham Publishing, London (1999)

Nicolas, Sir Nicholas Harris ed., *The Dispatches and Letters of Vice Admiral Lord Nelson,* vols. V–VII, Chatham Publishing, London (1998)

Oman, Carola, *Nelson,* Greenhill Books, London (1996)

Pocock, Tom, *Horatio Nelson,* Pimlico, London (1994)

_____, *The Terror Before Trafalgar: Nelson, Napoleon and the Secret War,* John Murray, London (2003)

Pope, Dudley, *England Expects: Nelson and the Trafalgar Campaign,* Chatham Publishing, London (1999)

Robinson, William, *Jack Nastyface: Memoirs of an English Seaman,* Chatham Publishing, London (2002)

Robson, Martin, *Battle of Trafalgar,* Conway Maritime Press, London (2005)

Schom, Alan, *Trafalgar: Countdown to Battle, 1803–1805,* Penguin Books, London (1992)

St Vincent, Earl of, *Letters of Admiral of the Fleet, the Earl of St Vincent whilst First Lord of the Admiralty, 1801–1804,* vol. 2, Navy Records Society, London (1927)

Sugden, John, *Nelson: A Dream of Glory, vol. I,* Jonathan Cape, London (2004)

Terraine, John, *Trafalgar,* Wordsworth Editions Ltd, London (1998)

Tracy, Nicolas, *Nelson's Battles: The Art of Victory in the Age of Sail,* Chatham Publishing, London (1996)

Tunstall, Brian, *Naval Warfare in the Age of Sail: The Evolution of Fighting Tactics, 1650–1815,* Conway Maritime Press, London (1990)

Vincent, Edgar, *Nelson: Love and Fame,* Yale University Press, New Haven, CT (2004)

Warwick, Peter, *Voices from Trafalgar,* David & Charles, London (2005)

Warner, Oliver, *Nelson's Battles,* Batsford, London (1965)

_____, *Trafalgar,* Pan Books, London (1966)

White, Colin, ed., *The Trafalgar Captains: Their Lives and Memorials,* Chatham Publishing, London (2005)

INDEX

Figures in **bold** refer to illustrations